RACE
PLAN

JEREMY BROWNE

REFORM

First published in Great Britain in 2014 by

Reform
45 Great Peter Street
London SW1P 3LT

ISBN 9781849547314
10 9 8 7 6 5 4 3 2 1

A CIP catalogue record for this book is available from the British Library.

Designed by Howdy

Printed and bound by
CPI Group (UK) Ltd, Croydon, CR0 4YY

Contents

The author

Jeremy Browne has been the Liberal Democrat Member of Parliament for Taunton Deane since 2005. He was a Minister of State in the Foreign and Commonwealth Office from 2010-12, where his specific responsibilities included Pacific Asia and Latin America. From 2012-13 he was a Minister of State in the Home Office. Jeremy lives in Taunton and London with his partner Rachel and their daughter Molly.

Acknowledgements

I am very grateful indeed for the tireless support of Tom Baycock in my Westminster office and of the Reform team: Callum Anderson, Harry Farmer, Andrew Haldenby, Freddie Heritage, Steph Lelievre, Rosie Olliver, Annie Reddaway, Ana Sofia-Monck, Lauren Thorpe, Tashi Warr and James Zuccollo.

Preface

The global order is being transformed as wealth and power spread beyond the established elite nations into the new emerging economies. The dominance of the leading Western countries that has existed since the Industrial Revolution is ending. Incrementally but remorselessly 'The Asian Century' is taking shape. The implications for Britain's prosperity, security and influence will be immense.

The nations of the industrialised West are now engaged in a race to secure a favourable position in this new world order. Those countries that adapt successfully to globalisation will continue to enjoy prosperity and wield influence. Those that do not will decline.

The question for Britain is whether we have the imagination, boldness and urgency needed to succeed. The stakes could not be higher: our private wealth, our public services, our international standing and our ability to protect and project our liberal values at home and abroad – all are at risk. Faced with these risks, caution and conservatism are, paradoxically, the greatest danger. We either embrace innovative change or live with the consequences of our inertia.

The shift of economic power to China and the other emerging powers would pose a big enough challenge to Britain in the best of times. Yet that challenge must now be confronted in the worst of times, as we emerge from the deepest recession in living memory, held back by a cautious and introspective political culture and weighed down by high levels of borrowing and debt.

Britain enters the global race with a number of advantages. We are a trading nation with a global disposition; we have a vibrant and inventive population; our elite education is among the best in the world; we have a proud tradition of freedom before the law; our language is the global language; we sit between East and West as a member of the world's largest single market.

But the financial crash of 2008 also exposed a number of significant structural weaknesses: a dangerously large deficit, an oversized and unresponsive public sector, high welfare bills, creaking infrastructure, a long tail of educational failure and the burgeoning costs of an ageing population.

Faced with these weaknesses, the key question is not *whether* Britain seeks to adapt to the challenge of globalisation but *how* we adapt.

———————

The changes Britain requires must work with, rather than against, the forces of globalisation, and go with, rather than against, the grain of our national character. That is why liberalism – pure, undiluted and authentic – provides the best guide for the years ahead.

Only authentic liberalism can unleash the attributes that Britain will need most: individuality, innovation, creativity, originality and a willingness to challenge stale thinking. And only authentic liberalism can position Britain to benefit from the market forces that drive globalisation and the internationalist politics that shape it.

We must champion our *economic* liberalism if we are to keep our markets open for business. A vibrant capitalism is lifting the living standards of billions of people around the world. Yet competition, choice, wealth creation and profit are, for many in Britain, seen as a problem rather than a template for success. That needs to change.

We must be committed to *personal* liberalism if we are to foster the creativity and innovation that feed off individual freedom. A misguided paternalism has entered our politics, but at the cost of stifling both freedom and personal responsibility. That too needs to change.

And we need to rediscover the true meaning of *social* liberalism. The era of big state social democracy ended with the financial crash of 2008. The task today is to push power, money, information and choice down to the individual citizen, so that everyone can enjoy the opportunities that a fortunate few take for granted.

We cannot afford the political procrastination that is too often our default mode when faced with big decisions. Instead of a new hub airport, we have a new hub airport commission. Instead of returning the top rate of tax from 50p to 40p, we uneasily split the difference at 45p. Instead of addressing the real causes of low wages – low productivity and educational failure – we pretend that artificial distortions of the labour market will painlessly make everyone wealthier.

Intrinsic to an authentic liberal mindset is the belief that, as a nation, we should look forward not back, and outward not inward; that we can build a future that is better than our past; and that we have the capacity to compete in, benefit from and contribute to the wider world. A nostalgic yearning for a Britain insulated from globalisation will only lead to marginalisation and failure. We need to have the confidence to look beyond such false comforts.

What does all this mean for our politics today?

It means liberating the talents of all our people, not just protecting the advantages of the privileged minority, to enable our country to realise its full potential.

It means fostering a culture that celebrates, rather than denigrates, wealth creation, enterprise and hard work; a smaller, more efficient state, with lower personal taxes.

It means supporting the free movement of goods, capital and labour that has enriched us and billions of others around the world.

It means spending only what we can afford to spend, and taking the hard decisions to turn wasteful day-to-day spending into productive long-term investment, particularly in skills and infrastructure.

It means recapturing the pioneering spirit of those who designed our systems of social welfare after the Second World War, so that we can re-cast our public services for the modern age.

And it means defining a clear and purposeful role for Britain in the world. We need to build new relationships and explore new markets. But above all, we need to protect and project our universally applicable liberal values of liberty, justice and human rights.

'The Global Race' will test the resolve of every nation. Some will fall short while others will achieve their ambitions for greater prosperity and influence. Britain needs a new and self-confident national attitude that refuses to accept failure and resolves to take the difficult decisions needed to succeed.

Britain needs a race plan. This is it.

Chapter one
The revolution is happening

I t was in a restaurant in Shanghai in 2008 that the full magnitude of what is happening struck me. It was then that I realised that all the assumptions I had held since childhood were becoming obsolete; that the whole world order was changing and would be utterly transformed within my working lifetime. It was disorientating but exhilarating. Above all, it was profoundly radicalising. When I flew back into Heathrow at the end of my visit, I looked at London, and at Britain, with fresh eyes, seeing my own country as visiting foreigners must see it. For the first time, I felt I fully understood the challenges we faced as a nation. My political outlook has not been the same since.

My father spent his whole career in the diplomatic service,

so I had the privilege from the beginning of seeing many different countries. But in my first five years as a Member of Parliament I travelled very little, only twice venturing outside Europe on parliamentary visits. Once was to the Democrat convention in Denver to see the nomination of Barack Obama as the Presidential candidate in 2008. The other trip was to Shanghai and neighbouring Suzhou. Despite the drama of being in the crowd of 84,000 people at the Mile High Stadium, it was the trip to China that made the bigger and more lasting impact.

I had never been to China before. I was 38. I had heard about the dramatic changes that were taking place there, and wanted to see what was happening. I realised that Shanghai was no more representative of China than New York is of America, but that made it more intriguing, not less. I wanted to see the change in its most dynamic and concentrated form. Even so, despite being forewarned, nothing I had read, or seen on television, properly prepared me for that moment in the Shanghai restaurant.

The Bund in Shanghai is the old mercantile row of buildings on the river. They once dominated the city and, despite being only about six stories high, their robust construction, combined with their historical significance, means they remain a memorable feature of Shanghai. The restaurant was on the top floor of one of these buildings. I was sitting opposite a British man who had lived in China for many years.

The view out of the window was absolutely dazzling. Across the river, fully illuminated against the night sky, was a Manhattan-like skyline. Indeed, if anything, it trumped Manhattan; the architecture was more audacious, the buildings newer, the lights brighter. "It's a remarkable view" said the man opposite. "But what is most amazing is that, a dozen years ago, there was nothing there".

That was the moment I first understood the pace of

the change. I had previously thought that, even in its most accelerated phases, urban development was essentially organic. Cities evolved over decades, with new bursts of growth reflecting periods of economic prosperity. Even when new sections were constructed, an extended period was required to put in place the planning permission, secure funding, put tenders out to architects, hire construction firms and sort out the necessary transport infrastructure.

The tallest towers across the river were a hundred stories high: even at a floor a fortnight, it would take four years to build each of those skyscrapers. Yet I was not being invited to admire a single spectacular building. I was looking at a full metropolis, where little more than a decade earlier there had been emptiness. And this was just one example. Across China, and across Asia, cities that most people in Britain have never even heard of were exploding in size. The audacity of the ambition was beyond anything I had contemplated before or been exposed to back at home. A full-scale economic revolution was taking place. And I was looking at it out of a restaurant window.

In that remarkable week my global political viewpoint was shifted off its axis. Anyone can read statistics about Chinese economic development, but there is no substitute for witnessing a revolution first-hand.

Another insight that remains imprinted in my mind was in Suzhou, a short journey from Shanghai. Our group was being shown the plans for the new section of the city. The scale was again awe-inspiring. The extension alone would, if built in Britain, become our second biggest city. Our hosts were keen to demonstrate that this would be a balanced community, not just a sprawling residential suburb.

So we were taken on a tour of a new university. It was

of particular interest to a British delegation because it was a joint venture between Liverpool University and Xi'an Jiaotong University from China. The facilities were impressive. As our tour with the Vice Chancellor came towards its conclusion, I looked out of the window at a substantial new building being constructed opposite. "Is that part of your university too?" I asked. "No, that's part of another university" he replied, very matter-of-factly. We all admired the vision of building two brand new universities simultaneously, side-by-side.

What was striking was not just the speed at which the extension to the city was being built, although it is worth reflecting on how long it might take us in Britain to build an urban area bigger than Birmingham. It was the fact the newly expanded city of Suzhou, once completed, would, we were told, be equipped with no fewer than seven universities. The scale of the intellectual ambition more than matched that of the physical ambition.

The third moment from that trip that drove home the significance of what was happening in China came in the Asian headquarters of BP, back in Shanghai. We were welcomed by two senior employees. The first, who was British, was the head of Asian operations for BP. The second, an American with a less corporate appearance, was the head of global innovation for BP.

It was logical that the head of Asian operations would be based in Shanghai, although still interesting that he was not in Hong Kong, Singapore or Tokyo. But it was less obvious why the head of global innovation would be there. It might have been more natural for him to be located at the company HQ in London, or in his home country of America.

To him it was obvious, however: "If you're responsible for innovation and change, you want to be in the place where change is happening fastest".

These three stories captured the essence of that week: dramatic physical change, dramatic intellectual change, and dramatic change full-stop. It was exhilarating to witness the dynamism, excitement and sense of almost limitless possibility that comes from being in a place where all of these changes are happening simultaneously. The Chinese were not just replicating what exists elsewhere, but aiming to surpass it. Their ambition was not just to catch up with the industrialised nations, but to overtake them.

In every area China is pushing the boundaries, and on a massive scale. This is not just about development in the conventional sense; it is about where the hungriest search for progress is located. It is about global power; not just national change. It is about which parts of the world are looking to the future and which parts are moored in the past.

In 2010 I became a Foreign Office Minister, with specific responsibility for Britain's relations with Asia and Latin America. My task was to engage with the parts of the world where change is happening fastest. I travelled constantly, not just to the developing giants like China, India and Brazil, but also to the countries in the next tier: South Korea, Indonesia, Mexico and Colombia.

What I observed on my travels was nothing less than a global economic revolution, the magnitude of which remains woefully underestimated and misunderstood in Britain. A seismic shift is taking place in world affairs. It will have the most profound impact on virtually every aspect of our lives.

The dominance of the Western nations, which began with the Industrial Revolution, will come to an end during my working life. The last time such as shift took place, when Britain surrendered its pre-eminent global position to the United States, it took place between two like-minded countries and established allies. It did not threaten the existing world order, or challenge the values and rules that underpinned it. The Americans modelled their systems on ours. They spoke our language. They shared our outlook.

Now all bets are off. This revolution may not feature much on our television screens, probably because it involves little violence or drama. It does not attract the cameras like the fall of the Berlin Wall or the attack on the World Trade Center. But it is taking place, incrementally but remorselessly and unstoppably. Every day China is more important than it was yesterday.

Just because the transformation is incremental does not mean that it is slow. Perhaps it is most easily understood by comparing it to the ageing process. When I look in the mirror I do not see a face that looks older than it was yesterday, although it is. The change is constant but gradual. But a portrait photo that is just three years old is subtly and recognisably different. After five years the difference is clear. After ten years we are obliged to change our passport photo.

This phenomenon is primarily about economic power, but from that flows political power, military power and, in time, even cultural power. After the Cold War, with victory for Western capitalism and democracy, we fast became accustomed to a global order rooted in the West. Power resided around the north Atlantic. The visual demonstration of this order was the photo-call for the leaders at a G8 summit. Joined by the President of the Commission of the European Union, the nine power-brokers stand in line. All of them represent Western domination – America, Canada, Britain, Germany, France, Italy, the EU, and now even Russia, with its European heritage, history and capital city – except one: Japan. The Japanese Prime Minister appears to be representing not just his own country but the whole of the rest of the world.

But that narrow G8 world is dissolving away. Instead a G20 world has emerged. Asia is much more heavily represented: China, India, Japan, South Korea, Indonesia, and, in an interesting shift in their national psychology, Australia. But it is also now a multi-polar model: South Africa, Argentina, Mexico – power is being diffused.

Leading this transformation, however, is China: the country with the world's biggest population and second biggest economy.

In my many conversations with Chinese Ministers, they were keen to stress that they are only travelling down the path that Britain had initially established. They frequently compared their progress in recent decades to the transformation over a comparable timescale of Britain following the Industrial Revolution. They observed the huge progress made by Victorian Britons who built railway infrastructure, imposing public buildings and millions of new houses. They admired the rapid urbanisation of Britain over that period, and the noble progress that was made in public sanitation, healthcare and education. They even, pointedly, noted how, at the equivalent stage in Britain's economic and social evolution, we had not yet felt able to embrace democracy or abolish the death penalty.

It is certainly true that peoples everywhere have followed a similar development pattern, from a life of subsistence, to organised agrarianism, to a rapid embrace of industrialisation and urbanisation. Victorian Britons travelled further down that path than any before them and their achievements must have been awesome to witness. But there are two big differences between what happened then and what is happening in China now: scale and context. What we did, they are doing much bigger. And, crucially, they are doing it in a much more networked, integrated and interdependent world. What is happening in China affects all of us.

They have already made startling progress on their remarkable journey.

In 1990, China had 147 kilometres of motorway. They started the National Trunk Highway System project, with the goal of increasing this to 35,000 kilometres by 2020. By 2007 they had already met this target, and revised it to 85,000 kilometres by 2020. This was surpassed in 2011[1].

In 1990 China had 0 kilometres of high-speed railway lines. By 2011 it had 10,000 kilometres[2].

In 1990 China's GDP was $357 billion. It is now $8.23 trillion – roughly *23 times* bigger. By 2024 China's GDP is predicted to become as high as $47 trillion – *131 times* larger than it was in 1990[3].

Then there is the investment too in human, as well as physical, capital. According to the British Council, 300 million people in China are learning or have learned to speak English. That is more than five times the population of England. By 2020, an estimated two billion people will be learning English worldwide[4]. English language training was the second most profitable business in China in 2005.

And it is not just the statistics that inspire awe. Chinese airports are cathedrals of modernity. Even the train stations feel like airports. When I visited Chongqing in 2011 I was told that the city had over a hundred buildings currently under construction that were taller than anything in Canary Wharf. And that is in a city already more than twice the size of London.

This remarkable development is pulling hundreds of millions of ordinary Chinese people away from extreme poverty.

Many still live materially squalid lives, but many others now have a standard of living which would have been unimaginable a generation ago.

In 1990 life expectancy in China was 69 years. Today it is 76 years. In 1990 infant mortality was 34 per 1,000 born. Today it is 15 per 1,000 born[5]. In 1990 the number of Chinese people who travelled to a foreign country was 980,000[6]. In 2012 it was 80 million[7].

Despite all of this, a worryingly large number of influential Western observers seem not to fully understand what is happening in China and across Asia, or what it will mean for us. Too many still characterise China as a "sweatshop" economy that is destined never to move up the value chain. The challenge of increased competition is blithely dismissed as a "race to the bottom".

It is hard to overstate the danger of such complacency. It is true that millions of Chinese people work in factories, earning low wages, to produce low-cost goods, like cheap children's toys, for Western consumers. No country has progressed from grinding poverty to being the most powerful nation on the planet without going through some intermediate stages. Every country needs to work its way up, and low-value activity is certainly better than no-value activity. But that is not the extent of their national ambition. They are not planning to halt their development just at the point where they export low-cost toys to us and we export high-tech, high-value products to them.

China's plan is more spectacular than some observers in Britain appear to comprehend. They want to manufacture the high-tech goods, and they are already doing so in greater quantities, but they also want to invent the next generation of higher-tech goods still. Their vision for their population is not entrenched penury while people in the West enjoy material prosperity. That is why they are investing so heavily in education and training: to build a work force with the knowledge and skills to be internationally competitive, and in time, to be global leaders.

The Chinese have the self-awareness to see their current limitations and the wisdom to seek to rectify them. They know that they are strong at manufacturing but weak at innovation and creativity. Their spectacular new buildings are often built by Chinese labourers but designed by European architects. They can see where the greatest value-added aspects of the work reside and that these do not currently match their strengths. So they are actively aspiring to adapt their educational models to incorporate more imaginative and lateral thinking. They are not sending their greatest young minds to the best Western universities like Oxford and Cambridge just for their private benefit. They are doing so as part of a systematic plan to upgrade their capacity for national growth.

Look at another aspect of added value – brands. There are no really dominant global Chinese brands, although Huawei (telecommunications) and Haier (white goods) are signs of what is to come. This shortfall, compared to, say, America, is an issue for China, because brands create money from nothing. Across Asia people in factories are manufacturing trainers for a few dollars a pair. They are cheap to make. They are then shipped around the world and sold by Western companies like Adidas and Nike at a huge mark-up. The companies can charge so much because consumers are not just buying a product; they are buying into a brand. Creating a brand is not easy. There are no manuals to follow or short cuts to take. But the Chinese are on the case, and they start with one major advantage: they have 1.3 billion people of their own before they even have to start enticing the consumers from elsewhere in the world. Once they have made progress in their own market, they will be well on their way. It is only a matter of time.

It may be comforting for Western politicians to paint a contrast between Chinese workers rooted to the bottom in "sweatshops" and Western people enjoying an entitlement to ever increasing affluence. But it is a false comfort.

China may be the engine room of the economic revolution that is reshaping our world, but there are many other countries making the same journey. Although the scale is smaller elsewhere, the progress is often even more remarkable.

When, as a Foreign Office Minister, I asked opinion-formers in aspirational developing countries which nation they used as a model to emulate, a disproportionately large number named South Korea. They were right to do so. The progress of South Korea is one of the greatest success stories in the history of human advancement.

When I was born in 1970, South Korea was a chronically poor country. It had a lower GDP per capita than North Korea, and was broadly comparable to the countries of East Africa. It was politically authoritarian and, in terms of its wider contribution and influence, globally insignificant.

In little more than a generation South Korea has leapt forward in every area and at a phenomenal pace. Back in 1962 South Korea's GDP was just $2.7 billion; in 1989 it was $230 billion; in 2007 it went through the trillion dollar barrier[8].

South Korea is home to businesses like Samsung, LG, Kia and Hyundai: powerful brands with global reach. They have increased dramatically their market share in both the development and the manufacture of high-value products like smart phones and flat screen televisions. It is not just Western nations that are seeing the impact of this surge: Japanese companies have also lost business to their South Korean rivals.

The GDP of South Korea has not only risen sharply, it has climbed with remarkable reliability and steadiness. There have not so far been the debilitating peaks and troughs that have characterised our own economic development; just a constant upwards trajectory. And efforts are being made to sustain the momentum, with a focus now on attracting global-standard scientists to power the research and innovation necessary to secure future prosperity.

This economic success would be impressive in isolation, but it has been accompanied by political and cultural advances every bit as extraordinary. South Korea has made the successful transition internally to being a democracy and open society. On the international political stage, the Secretary General of the United Nations is a South Korean. It is an important G20 country, in part because it is now the fifteenth biggest economy in the world[9], and in part because its role-model status is starting to give South Korea greater confidence in its international interactions.

Economic and political progress has also been accompanied by a rise in South Korea's soft power. The 1988 Olympics was just the first of a number of high-profile global sporting events to be awarded to South Korea, followed by the 2002 football World Cup (jointly with Japan), the 2011 World Athletics championships and the 2018 winter Olympics. It is an impressive list for a country with a smaller population than Britain.

On my visit to Pacific Asia in 2008 I sat in the reception of a Shanghai hotel one evening listening to a Chinese entertainer singing Elvis songs. Although the manifestations of economic progress were all around me, I reflected that it would be many decades before anyone would sit in a Western bar listening to a Western performer singing an Asian song.

Yet it was only five years before the world was introduced to Psy, a South Korean singer whose 'Gangnam Style' video has been watched almost two billions times on Youtube – a record. Virtually every child in Britain knows the 'Gangnam Style' dance. I have even been to an event in my Taunton Deane constituency where the Mayor and Mayoress were gamely obliged to join in with a rendition.

Psy is proof that Asian countries can export popular culture. He is massive in South Korea, of course, and across Asia, but what is significant is his reach into Europe and America. Previously, cultural exports flowed almost exclusively from West to East: The Beatles, Madonna, Coca-Cola and James Bond. That remains the main direction of travel, but Psy has shown that the cultural tide can flow in the other direction. It is often said that this will be 'The Asian Century'. For that to be true, Asia needs to export more than manufactured goods. America is the most powerful country in the world because it has the biggest economy and the biggest military, but also because it has the greatest cultural reach.

The Psy phenomenon is interesting for two other reasons. South Korea produces an endless stream of identikit pop bands, some of which are very popular domestically, but none of which has had a wider impact. Psy is older and fatter than they are, but he is authentic. A country with an uncertain feel for international trends can try and export mass popular culture but it is unlikely to get the formula right. A more culturally confident country can unwittingly provide the conditions to incubate natural and non-formulaic mass popular culture. South Korea has made this transition.

The other observation is about the subject of the song: gently ridiculing the opulence and pretensions of the residents of Gangnam in Seoul. It says much about how far South Korea has travelled since the poverty of the 1970s that it now boasts a district of its capital city associated with gaudy displays of wealth. It says much about how far it has travelled in terms of its cultural self-confidence that it can make light-hearted fun of it. And it says much about how far it has travelled in terms of its international reach that we can all share in the fun.

I will not describe in detail the progress being made in every fast-developing country in the world because the point has been made, except to say this: it is happening on many different levels in many different places. It is emphatically not merely about low-level manufacturing in "sweatshops" across China and some of the poorer South East Asian countries like Cambodia or Laos.

Some of the progress is unpredictable and counter-intuitive. It is not surprising, for example, that Brazil sees itself as moving beyond being the dominant South American country to becoming a genuine international player. Its relaxed self-confidence (at least on the surface) will manifest itself at the 2014 football world cup and 2016 Olympics. The Brazil brand – flowing football, sunny beaches, beautiful women, carnivals and spectacular rainforests – is about as attractive as any country can hope to possess.

But Brazil is not content, sensibly, to trade purely on its existing brand strengths. It is seeking a global role in more hard-headed areas of progress. Brazil's science base, for example, is now internationally significant. Increasingly the established powerhouse nations in medical research are looking at mutually beneficial partnership arrangements with the Brazilians.

Indian development, once synonymous in the British mind with off-shored call centres, continues to move up the value-chain, and is now often associated instead with specialist IT contractors in high growth cities like Bangalore.

There is a risk, as well, that the British discussion of the emerging economies focuses too narrowly on the BRICs – Brazil, Russia, India and China (some say the 'S' also includes South Africa). As the South Korean illustration shows, the BRICs may be the biggest of the emerging economies, but many other fast rising countries are enjoying impressive results but receive much less attention.

Indonesia is the fourth most populous country in the world and the sixteenth biggest economy. It has a population of 249 million and is the only G20 country in South East Asia. Jakarta is a significant Asian hub city. It only takes 10 per cent of Indonesians to achieve sufficient wealth to become middle-class consumers for the country to be powerful attractive to Western investors.

Mexico is the eleventh most populous country in the world and the fourteenth biggest economy. It also has the major advantage of bordering the biggest economy in the world. Mexico primarily looks to America for business, but it is also instinctively outward looking in its mindset. The Mexicans are routinely critical of the Brazilians, who they regard as too inclined to protectionism.

Mexico's formal relationship with like-minded 'Pacific Rim' countries (Chile, Colombia, Peru, Panama and Costa Rica) adds up to a formidable economic block comparable in scale to Brazil. Colombia, with the second largest population in South America after Brazil, is unequivocally internationalist in its economic perspective, and has enjoyed solid and sustained annual growth.

The point is this: the shift in the global order is multi-dimensional. China is the breathtaking example; South Korea arguably the most impressive model. But it goes wider. I anticipate this will indeed be 'The Asian Century'. But economic power is moving south as well as east. The opportunities for growth will open up for countries right around the world that can get their governance structures right.

If the story of the last twenty years is awe-inspiring, the projections for the next twenty years are no less dramatic. I am 43 years old – roughly half-way through a typical working life time. By the time I retire, the still emerging economies will have emerged. The still changing world order will have been utterly transformed.

Again, the numbers are instructive:

Up until 1990 Europe's share of global GDP was about 30 per cent. In 2010 it was 26 per cent[10]. By 2030 Europe's share of global GDP is predicted to fall to just 12 per cent[11].

The current size of the global economy is approximately $72 trillion but the real expansion is yet to come. The rapid future growth will come disproportionately from Asia. By 2030 the most dramatic predictions forecast that China will have 28 per cent of global GDP, America 18 per cent and India 11 per cent (a level only just below that of all the European countries combined)[12].

Even if these growth forecasts prove flattering to the Asian economies, the direction of travel is clear. By 2060 it is estimated that 57 per cent of global GDP will be generated by countries currently outside the OECD[13]. That in turn will finance a lot more investment – in education, public services and infrastructure – that will drive further prosperity.

And the transformative effect is not just measurable in cash. The world population reached seven billion in 2012. It is forecast to be 9.7 billion by 2050. Where will these extra people be located? Not in Europe, where the population is forecast to decline by 14 per cent by 2050[14]. The growth will predominantly occur in Asia, where the increase alone will be greater than the current population of Europe.

Population growth is not without potential problems: providing enough housing, access to clean water and food, energy supplies, environmental protection, education and physical infrastructure. But overcome those challenges, and all those extra people will provide huge economic firepower: hundreds of millions more workers producing more goods, providing more services and generating more wealth.

The other crucial aspect of these population changes is not the absolute numbers but the age profile of the populations in different countries.

Dependency ratios – the ratio of working age people to dependents (children and the elderly) – are heading into uncharted territory across the developed economies, as the number of old people rises and the birth rate slows.

The most arresting example is Japan, which has a population profile much closer to the Western economies than to its Asian neighbours.

In 1970 Japan had 48 dependents per 100 working people. It has now already reached 60. The Japanese population is growing older at a remarkable rate. Today Japan's population is 127 million, but some estimates predict it will fall below 90 million by 2060 as the birth rate continues to decline[15]. If that happens, Japan will have seen its total population contract by a third in just two generations, leaving behind a much older population. In 2013 Japan became the first country in the world to sell more nappies for old people than for babies.

Although not quite as drastic, the same trend in dependency ratios are being seen across advanced Western economies. Britain's picture is less stark than many, but our dependency ratio is still projected to rise from 54 today to 62 in 2030. Germany's ratio is set to rise from 52 to 70; France's from 56 to 66. Italy and Spain, meanwhile, will see their dependency ratios deteriorate at an even faster rate[16]. By 2050, they are projected to join Japan in having ratios above 100, meaning there will be more people economically inactive, than active, in all three countries.

Of course the fact we in the West are living so much longer is, in many ways, a cause for celebration. Two of my grandparents have died, aged 87 and 90. The other two are still alive, aged 93 and 97. When I was born in 1970 there were 149,000 people in Britain over the age of 90; today there are 476,000, and the numbers continue to rise[17]. This is a great human advance, and it would be wrong just to see it in terms of cold economic calculations.

But nor can we dismiss the value of these ratios in providing a guide to future economic prospects. There are other factors at play – good governance, unexpected economic shocks, education standards, natural disasters and many more – but population demographics are a significant crystal ball.

With Western economies heading into uncharted territory, China is predicted to remain stable over the next two decades (although their birth control restrictions point towards future problems), while India and Brazil are forecast to actually improve slightly as the number of working age people grows faster than the number of dependents.

Many of the smaller emerging economies will benefit from similar demographic advantages. Take Vietnam, for example. The population of Vietnam is 92 million, the fourteenth highest in the world[18], but its GDP per capita, at $1,753, is comparatively very low, only the 131st highest in the world.

There are a number of factors which make Vietnam look like an interesting prospect for Western investors. It borders China, the second biggest economy in the world, and is well located close to Japan, South Korea and within the ASEAN group of South

East Asian nations. It has links, for colonial reasons, with France and, somewhat counter-intuitively, America. As a Foreign Office Minister, it was evident that Vietnam was one of the most energetic countries in Asia when it came to seeking to forge stronger relations with Britain.

Vietnam has a surprisingly well educated workforce for such a relatively poor country – 93 per cent of Vietnamese people over the age of 15 can read and write[19] – and a strong work ethic. Ho Chi Minh City is an increasingly energetic and significant Asian business hub.

And this is the key point: the median age of a Vietnamese person is 29; their dependency ratio is only 41; and – like Indonesia, Thailand, South Korea, Mexico, and Colombia – its dependency ratio is projected to still be below 50 in 2030, compared with a projected European average of 60[20].

The only reasonable conclusion is that the opportunities for continued economic growth in Vietnam, as in much of Asia and Latin America, are very strong. They will experience set-backs along the way, and must overcome some significant structural problems, but the fundamentals are in place.

We like to talk about how we now live in a globalised world, but the truth is we are only in the foothills of globalisation. Fifty years from now people will laugh at the conceit that we had, in 2014, reached a new plateau in global economic affairs. We are still on a steep upwards curve. So far globalisation has been largely about what the Western countries have done to the rest of the world – outsourcing our manufacturing and lower-skilled service jobs. In the coming years, as globalisation accelerates and trade proliferates, new interdependencies, alliances and tensions will emerge. And underneath it all, one clear trend will continue: wealth will move south and east, from the old world to the new, changing the balance of global power completely and irrevocably.

In 1914 the Panama Canal opened. It must have felt like the start of a dramatic new era – because it was. In this centenary year, 2014, the new Panama Canal is nearing completion, not as a replacement for the old one, but alongside it. It will take much bigger ships and facilitate more global trade. Its opening too will feel like the start of a new era – because it is.

———————————

I am conscious, as I describe these trends, of the need not to underestimate either the weaknesses of the emerging powers or the strengths of the Western economies.

China has yet to resolve the dangerous contradiction inherent in granting its people significant economic freedom while continuing to deny them the political freedoms that we in the West take for granted. The Chinese economy is also vulnerable to debt-financed assets deflating in value with a knock-on slowdown in overall economic growth.

India has the world's biggest democracy, but it often struggles with political incoherence, religious instability and administrative complexity.

The countries of Latin America are held back by a woefully inadequate physical infrastructure, the serious weakness in some cases of their governance, and chronic problems with drugs and violent crime.

All of them, meanwhile, remain home to millions of the world's poorest people, for whom the next meal remains the most pressing concern.

So, no, I do not underestimate the weaknesses of the emerging powers or the strengths of the Western economies. But I do worry that we in Britain – in our public consciousness, in our political discourse, and in the assumptions that underpin our policy making – are guilty of the opposite: underestimating the strengths of the emerging powers and the weaknesses of our own economies.

The purpose of this book is to help shake us out of our dangerous complacency, to engender a greater sense of political urgency, and to suggest some of the corrective measures we must take to both protect ourselves and to succeed during a period of revolutionary global realignment.

The change is happening. We will either adapt and prosper, or fail to and decline.

Chapter two
What has it got to do with us?

From the vantage point of Britain, looking across at Asia or Latin America, it is easy and tempting to imagine that the huge on-going upheaval in the global order need not be of direct concern to us. Sure, Shanghai is expanding, South Korean living standards are rising, and science is driving the Brazilian economy up the value chain – but why should we care? Most Britons will never visit China, South Korea or Brazil and have a limited interest in what is happening many thousands of miles away. The big changes in the world feel far removed from the day-to-day concerns of the typical British citizen.

British politicians generally reflect this view. The American Congressman Tip O'Neill famously observed that "all politics is local", and certainly, in a democracy, the preferred method for engaging with voters is to focus relentlessly on the immediate and the tangible: prices in the shops, the cost of gas and electricity, or the state of local schools and hospitals.

These bread-and-butter issues are certainly of great importance to the electorate. They are how most people measure their standard of living and their prospects for future prosperity. And, in a democracy, what matters to voters, matters to politicians. Any elected politician who is unconcerned about events in his or her own constituency will not remain an elected politician for long.

But the new reality is that the immediate concerns of our everyday lives cannot plausibly be disaggregated from the remarkable developments that are happening elsewhere in the world. They are, in fact, linked to a far greater extent than ever before, to a degree which would have been unimaginable to Tip O'Neill when he coined his phrase in the 1930s.

Today the fastest and most spectacular changes in the world are happening elsewhere – not just far removed from our country, but also from our continent. We cannot afford the luxury of ignoring these changes or assuming that they do not apply to us. When, 150 years ago, the most rapid progress in the world was happening in Britain, the onus was on others to spend more time looking at us. The Americans, as the dominant world power today, are notoriously insular, quick to assume that everyone can learn from them and that they have little to learn from others. That assumption certainly no longer applies to us, and increasingly it will not apply to the Americans either.

In our interconnected world, what happens at the local level, or even at the national level, can only be fully understood by reference to what is happening at the global level. And increasingly, the global forces that shape our lives – that affect the jobs we do, the goods we buy, the fuel we use, the houses we can afford, even the football teams we support – are unleashed thousands of miles away, on the other side of the world. And these global forces can be more powerful by far than the national politicians we elect.

This fact is a source of some considerable discomfort for national politicians, for it requires them to accept a degree of weakness to which no elected representative will easily admit. Faced with public and media demands that 'something must be done' about a matter of pressing concern, it is a rare politician who confesses to an inability to rectify a problem. So actions are taken which, at best, may delay or deflect the effects of these global forces, but without fundamentally altering them.

Yet with every such intervention, the sense is communicated that the British Government has a level of control which is impossible in a globalised economy. It suits both the Government of the day and the official opposition to maintain this illusion. It is, perhaps, not surprising that the electorate feels short-changed when politicians, having promised to tackle a problem over which they have little or no control, are unable, in the end, to deliver the outcome they promised.

But perhaps the greatest problem for politicians, particularly in a democracy, is that it is never an appealing prospect to be the deliverer of unwelcome home-truths. The changes happening across the world will shape nearly every aspect of our lives. Some of the consequences will be positive, but many may not be, and our need to respond to a radically different global situation will require us to reassess almost every established orthodoxy about our politics and public services. As people are inevitably unsettled by change, even if they know the change is unavoidable, it is easier not to dwell on it too much.

So anyone watching our debates in the House of Commons

could be forgiven for believing that the global revolution is a side-show, of little consequence for us. But the opposite is true. Not only are the consequences of the shift in economic power already being felt, but they will become magnified as that shift becomes more pronounced.

For better or for worse, the global economic revolution will exert an ever more powerful influence over our decision-making calculations in the years to come. Our politicians may hold fewer levers of control in their hands than previously, but we are not powerless in the face of globalisation. We have to be realistic about what we can both prevent and achieve, and then be resolute in making the right long-term decisions. The response that we formulate will determine our future success.

The economic crash of 2008 would have been very damaging at any time, but it came at a particularly unfortunate point in the shift of global power from west to east. Our deficiencies were exposed at precisely the moment when the economic competition was shifting into a higher gear.

In the 1970s Britain suffered from chronically bad governance. Our industries were uncompetitive and plagued by strikes. Then, the Government did the opposite of what was needed; embracing the concept of the three-day-week and setting prices in consultation with the trade unions.

Britain was left badly exposed, and other countries were presented with an opportunity to take advantage of our weakness. It was our good fortune that the pool of industrialised countries able to exploit that weakness was so small, and that some of our competitors suffered from some of the same problems that beset us. The Germans, the Japanese and a few other advanced economies were able to make relative advances, but we were largely cushioned from the full consequences of our hopelessness.

Back then there was no roaring Chinese economy. The total GDP of China was smaller than that of Belgium. The Indian economy was sealed off and dysfunctional, while the other Asian economies, outside Japan, were minute. The Latin American economies were also tiny, and the continent was ill-served by a host of disastrous authoritarian governments. Meanwhile, the Soviets were busy demonstrating that, despite the havoc caused by socialism in Britain, it was possible for a country to perform even more disastrously if the economic medicine was administered in a yet more concentrated form.

As a result, we were spared, by accident rather than design, a worse economic fate. The consequences of addressing our economic malaise were still hugely painful, and some linger to this day, but, like an unsuccessful team in a league with no system of relegation, we were largely insulated from the consequences of our failings.

That is emphatically not the case today. If we cannot get our act together and perform to our full potential, the consequences will be far more severe.

This, of course, is not just true of Britain. It applies to all of the western industrialised economies. Past performance is no longer a reliable guide to future success. In today's globalised economy, there is no divine right to remain relatively prosperous.

I fear that the European Union, and a good number of its member states, fails to grasp this central truth. Our continent accounts for a rapidly shrinking proportion of the global economy. Right across Europe, we need to think about how we can be more globally competitive. Instead, in an eerie echo of the British political debate in the 1970s, some European leaders, and a larger number of would-be leaders, propose policies that would do the exact opposite.

It is just not feasible, for example, to maintain a retirement age of 60, or even lower, in any country where life expectancy has risen dramatically, the level of public debt is high, many pension schemes are unfunded or under-funded, and the dependency ratio is worsening. There is not an inalienable right to a comfortable retirement lasting several decades. If there were, people in Asia would all be signing up for the same option. The money has first to be earned, then saved.

And it is not feasible either to demand generous pensions and high quality public services, while imposing stifling constraints on wealth creation. The concept of the maximum working week could just about be sustained if all our competitors agreed to the same limit. But just having limits within the European Union reveals a dated belief that we can create and hoard prosperity without the need to be as industrious as people elsewhere in the world. If it were possible to enjoy an affluent lifestyle without having to work to generate the affluence, people in Asia would be signing up for that option as well.

We are in a much more fluid, much more competitive world. If we do not have the skills and work ethic in Britain to do the jobs, the jobs will go elsewhere. If we do not make Britain attractive for investors, investment will go elsewhere. This is just the beginning. Globalisation is in its infancy.

Greater population movements mean that, even if we succeed in keeping jobs and investment in Britain, we cannot be certain that those jobs will be filled by British workers. This crunch has already been felt it many lower-skilled areas of employment. In London, for example, the staff at the seemingly unlimited number of Prêt a Manger sandwich shops are almost always unfailingly friendly and, even more noticeably, hardly ever British. But the crunch is not confined to relatively low paid, unskilled jobs. Immigrant populations tend to start at the bottom and work their way up over successive generations. Now, added to that, are the globally flexible managerial class, able to slot straight into senior positions in a new country.

Premier League football provides a case in point. Many of the managers are foreign. They operate in an international employment market. Jose Mourinho, the Chelsea manager and a Portuguese national, has moved from Portugal to England to Italy to Spain and back to England. His players are recruited from across the globe. Even the owners are operating in a global market: Americans at Manchester United, Liverpool and Arsenal; the Abu Dhabi ruling family at Manchester City; a Russian at Chelsea.

When I was a boy these clubs were resolutely British. They had Scottish and Irish players, but those from further afield were an exotic novelty. That was the 1970s, when Britain existed in a much more limited pool of advanced industrial nations, before globalisation began.

The football was also of a worse standard then, and the commercial scope of the leading football clubs was risible. Now they are global brands. Manchester United, Arsenal and Chelsea have a huge reach, particularly in Asia where, for commercial reasons, they now tour in the pre-season period. Liverpool, despite being without a league title for over twenty years, and with a dated stadium in a poorer part of Britain, remain in the elite cadre of clubs because of the continued resonance of their brand in Asian markets.

Even a modestly successful club like Everton offer an insight into the Asian-orientated transformation of English football in a globalised economy. Their sponsor, Chang, is a popular beer in

Thailand. The beer is rarely sold in Britain, but Chang are not aiming their sponsorship at the British market. They are putting their name on Everton's shirt because that is a guaranteed way to reach the domestic Thai market, where English Premier League football is extremely popular.

For Chang, Everton's limited success is a positive attraction. Sponsorship of the most successful teams, who feature in the Champions League, is much more expensive. Yet Champions League matches kick-off at 7.45pm – 2.45am in Thailand – which is hopeless for their domestic television market. Everton are therefore perfect for their purposes: easily good enough not to get relegated; rarely quite good enough to qualify for the Champions League. The majority of their matches kick-off at 3.00pm on a Saturday – 10.00pm in Thailand – ideal for their domestic television market.

Premier League football represents the globalisation phenomenon in microcosm. British employees are competing in a much tougher labour market, and many who would previously have secured jobs now struggle to do so. But for those who can compete in this internationalised labour market, the financial rewards have never been higher, while the product offered to consumers has never been better. Nor is that product any longer just 'ours'. It is packaged, sold and bought, in all its dimensions, by people from around the world. Many people are nostalgic for the way English football used to be, although if match day attendances and pay TV subscription levels are anything to go by, many more are not. Either way, there is no going back.

This is a glimpse into the future: greater movement of labour, capital and goods; more intense competition; a greater emphasis on quality and branding; the greatest rewards to those who can provide an attractive proposition to international investors. The task before us is not to stop the future happening; it is to recognise the nature of the challenge, and then adapt in order to survive and thrive.

Globalisation is causing economic waves which are washing up on every shore. The most unsettling impact is that of inward migration on labour markets, public services and housing, which is why the issue is the focus of so much public, media and political attention. But that is only one dimension.

The race for natural resources is a case in point. Global demand is rising, driving up prices and creating a greater impetus to further increase supply.

Chinese investment in Africa is changing the outlook of a continent whose primary external relationships were previously with former European colonial powers.

The Australian economy has been turbo-charged by a surge in demand for the minerals that sit below their vast and empty continental country. It has now grown for a remarkable 21 consecutive years, even riding out the global financial crash of 2008 largely unscathed. Public unease in Australia has instead focused on the unbalancing of the economy, with the boom in mining overshadowing other sectors where wages have failed to rise at the same pace. Unbalanced economic growth does cause problems, but it is not a bad problem to have when the other advanced economies have suffered from several years of little or no economic growth at all.

The race for resources has put Australia in an envious economic position. Its public debt, as a percentage of its GDP, is just 27 per cent. The contrast with Britain (90 per cent) and America (106 per cent), let alone countries like Italy (127 per cent) is stark[21]. Ten years ago Australia had a GDP per capita of $23,446, compared to Britain's $31,153. Today Australia's is $67,036 and Britain's is $38,514[22]. Big changes are happening over small time frames.

Some relatively obscure countries are suddenly finding themselves the focus of attention due to their rare mineral wealth. Bolivia has many charms, but it has one in particular for China: lithium. The sustained economic growth of Chile, the richest per capita country in South America, is due in part to good economic decisions, but it too is fuelled by mining.

And while it is difficult to predict accurately future oil and gas prices, few forecasters can see anything other than continued growth in demand and upward pressure on prices, albeit with fluctuations along the way.

That is keenly felt by British motorists and by every British household when the utility bills arrive. The British Government can relieve pressure at the margins by varying the tax levied, but it cannot alter the fundamental shift in global demand. In 1970 there were 250 million cars on the world's roads. In 1986 there were 500 million. Today there are over a billion, and nearly all of them run on fossil fuel[23].

The need to generate power is further increased as hundreds of millions of extra people rise into more energy reliant lifestyles. In 1985 just 7 per cent of Chinese urban families, and 0.1 per cent of rural families, owned a fridge. By 2007 this had risen to 95 per cent of urban families and 26 per cent of rural families[24]. That is a lot of extra fridges to keep cold. The Western countries, of course, continue to consume far more energy per person, but the demand for fridges in countries like Britain has plateaued. In China, even after this remarkable surge in demand, there are still hundreds of millions more people striving to afford these goods.

It is this fast rising demand that is driving the growth in

the emission of greenhouse gases that are having such a profound effect on the global atmosphere. It is both unrealistic and wrong to seek to frustrate the ambitions of billions of people across Asia, Africa and Latin America to enjoy the material comforts that we have come to take for granted in the West, but the fact remains that we need to find ways of meeting that extra demand without causing environmental havoc. This is one of the greatest challenges facing humankind. The race for unlimited, clean, green energy has already started. Britain should be at the forefront of that race.

It is interesting to note that the Chinese, and other Asian countries, are themselves alert to the potential for expanding the use of renewable resources. The crude portrayal of China in the Western media is of a highly polluted country that is building ever more coal and gas fired power stations with a blithe disregard for the consequences. But that tells only part of the true story. The Chinese calculation is that, with so many technologies still in their infancy, they need an iron in every fire. They are building more conventional and nuclear power stations at a bewildering rate, but they are also making considerable investments in renewable energy. China now generates almost three times more electricity from renewable sources every year than the entire annual energy consumption of Britain.

The endless hunt for raw materials is also manifesting itself in the unlikeliest of ways. Soaring demand for metal has seen prices rise, creating a hot global market for metal, especially higher value varieties like copper. The British Government has had to introduce fairly draconian legislation to regulate the domestic scrap metal market to try and reduce the incentive for thieves to strip lead off church roofs and steal the copper wiring from the railway network. Most people sitting on a late-running commuter train would not immediately think that their delay had been caused, however indirectly, by the changes taking place in Asia. But they would be wrong.

High end residential and commercial property is another example of a scarce commodity for which there is a fast growing global market, forcing prices ever higher. And it is here, in the most exclusive apartments and houses, in the most desirable neighbourhoods, in the world's most booming cities, that we can find the visible clues about where wealth is being concentrated and where people anticipate it will be generated in the future.

A home in central London's most sought after postcodes is now within reach of a rising number of very wealthy people from around the world. London is a financial centre and a vibrant cultural hub where property rights and the rule of law are respected. This makes it an attractive place to live, and an even more attractive place to invest.

As a result, London's housing market has become semi-disconnected from the majority of the city's population. Average earnings in England would stand at £55,296 – £29,000 higher than the actual level – had wages risen at the same pace as house prices over the last 15 years[25]. In London, the disparity is far greater still, and will almost certainly grow further as demand continues to rise faster than supply.

The prospect of owning your own home, which in previous generations seemed attainable for large numbers of people, has become a seemingly impossible dream for many younger people today. That is why delivering a step change in house building is vital if we are to honour the unwritten social contract between the generations and extend to the young the ladder of opportunity that their parents and grandparents have already climbed.

On the upside, the increasing demand from people around the world to have a presence in London is also fuelling a period of great investment and prosperity in our capital city. London has always had a certain energy, but the dreariness and architectural brutality of my childhood is giving way to a renaissance era of new building, driven by wealthy companies and individuals. I like the Shard, and the peculiar designs of the new towers in the City, but that is a matter of taste. What is beyond dispute is that a lot of money is pouring into London to build them. And this period is only just beginning: Battersea, Elephant and Castle and many other neglected parts of the capital are all now being developed. We are still in the foothills of globalisation.

Meanwhile, in major hub cities and aspirant hub cities elsewhere in the world, the changes to the skylines are, in many cases, even more spectacular. In the Gulf States, and in cities across China, grand statements of wealth and economic intent are rising from the ground.

I first visited America in 1989, as a nineteen year old. It did not cross my mind that the tallest buildings in the world would be anywhere other than America. I paid to go to the top of the tallest – Sears Tower in Chicago – and the second tallest – the World Trade Center in New York. Remarkably, at that point, the Empire State Building, despite being almost sixty years old, was still the third tallest building in the world – an indication of the slow pace of change then compared to the bewildering pace of change today.

For forty years, Sears Tower remained the tallest building in America. Only now have the Americans built a taller building, on the site of the old World Trade Center, and that happened only because of the appalling events of 9/11. But it is not the tallest building in the world. Far from it. The new One World Trade Center is the ninth tallest building in the world. And with new skyscrapers rising right now, it will not be long before America drops out of the top ten altogether.

Some will say this hardly matters. Why make a fuss over a hundred-storey building when two fifty-storey buildings provide just as much office space? But it mattered greatly to the Americans when they did have the tallest building. When I went up Sears Tower in 1989, the fact that it was the tallest building in the world was a big deal. The competition then was between Chicago and New York. Much like their domestic sports, this was branded as a global race, but all the participants were American. The message was clear: America is the biggest, wealthiest, most dynamic, most ambitious country in the world. America could do what other countries could not. And I did not doubt that for a moment.

A few years ago, at a business event in Asia, one attendee summed this change up for me: "Jeremy", he said, "I can tell you all you need to know about succeeding in business in the world today". He paused for effect. "It's Shanghai, Mumbai, Dubai – or bye-bye".

Although the consequences of economic global realignment are substantial, and although it is clearly true that Britain's share of world wealth is falling sharply, I am conscious of not being too bleak when considering how the global revolution will impact on our prosperity and relationships.

There are great opportunities for British businesses to export to new markets. In Asia in particular, there has already been a huge rise in the numbers of consumers with real purchasing power. British businesses that previously focused their attention on our domestic market, and then on our near European neighbours, can now realistically look much further afield.

Employees of these companies will be subject to increased

global competition for their jobs, but their roles will now often be more diverse, stimulating and lucrative. This need not apply only to big, established businesses. Surprisingly small, niche companies are finding a foothold in corners of the world which would have been off the business radar a generation ago.

As companies put down roots in different parts of the world, the employee opportunities also expand. More people, seizing an opportunity to transfer within their own company, are spending periods of time working elsewhere in the world, learning about new cultures and languages.

The wider opportunities for exploration are also expanding. Already over 700,000 British people live elsewhere in the European Union[26], benefiting from the rules allowing us to work and reside across the continent. And increasing numbers of people are living further afield: over a million in Australia, for example, and 600,000 in Canada[27].

Extended residency remains comparatively rare, but globalisation has brought the foreign holiday within reach of most families. It is much rarer now to meet a Briton who has never been abroad, and increasingly people are travelling much further afield. Last year 800,000 Britons visited Thailand alone[28].

And, in case we think our increased appetite for travel is exceptional, the statistics for the number of people visiting Britain from around the world are no less impressive.

As the Chinese middle class grows, so the number of people with the ability and inclination to explore the wider world has shot up. In 2012,, 210,000 Chinese visitors came to Britain[29]. They want to see Big Ben, Stratford-on-Avon and taste Scottish whisky in its original setting. A more imaginative visa system will provide far more opportunities to open up this lucrative tourism market.

But it would be limiting to see this new phenomenon in

purely economic terms. Globalisation has the power to enrich us culturally as well as financially. The people that embrace the new opportunities for social and intellectual exchange with the greatest enthusiasm will be the ones that make the greatest advances in the decades ahead. Insularity is the route to marginalisation.

There is no reason why our close allies of the future cannot be drawn from a bigger pool of countries. Over previous decades, for reasons of geographic proximity, history and culture, we have tended to develop are strongest working relationships with other European countries and with the English speaking countries of the Commonwealth like Canada, Australia and New Zealand. We should stay on good terms with all of these allies, but there is no reason to stop there. A world where Britain has closer connections with, for example, Mexico, Turkey and South Korea, will be a safer and more prosperous world.

Increased prosperity in Asia has produced the greatest leap forward for the greatest number of people of any time in history. It is inspiring and exhilarating to behold.

Since 1990, 500 million people in China alone have been lifted out of extreme poverty (living on less than $1 a day)[30]. In India, appalling diseases like polio, widely apparent when I first visited in 1989, have been virtually eradicated. And across the poorest parts of the world, unprecedented numbers of people now have access to clean water, shelter, medicine and education. Squalor and wretchedness are being replaced by dignity and optimism.

For some, this progress has only been possible because of international aid, with Britain one of the most generous donor countries. There are many children in the world today who have been spared lifelong disability because of British help. They may grow up grateful that Britain gave them the opportunity to live fulfilling lives, free from disability and poverty, and that may benefit us in the future, but even if they do not, we should be proud that we did the right thing.

More significant than aid though, has been trade, the growth of which has allowed countries to generate the wealth needed to better help their own populations. Decent housing, proper sanitation, vaccination programmes, healthy food, clean water, education – they all cost money. The economic liberation of China and India in particular, as the two most populous countries, has generated billions of extra dollars which have started to raise the living standards of their people. Anyone doubting the moral virtue of liberal economics should spend a couple of minutes comparing the lives of North Koreans and South Koreans.

The truth is that this progress does, over time, benefit Britain. But ultimately, I welcome these advances as a human being, not as a self-interested Briton.

And once countries reach a higher level of economic and educational development, the potential opportunities for humanity are vast.

I would be proud if the cure for cancer was discovered by a British scientist. With the second greatest number of Nobel prizes after America, our country has made a hugely disproportionate contribution to human development. But I do not mind that much who finds the cure. There are great fields of knowledge that humans have yet to conquer and terrible medical conditions that we have yet to vanquish. The more countries with the financial clout and the scientific capacity to contribute to this shared endeavour, the better.

———————————

The effects of globalisation, both positive and negative, described thus far will become more apparent in the coming years as the changes I have described gather pace. And, if we understand the nature of these changes and prepare for them, the consequences can largely be positive.

But there is one question to which we do not yet have an answer; a question that stands out above all others, for it goes to the very heart of what the Asian Century will mean for each and every one of us. And it is this: is China simply further back on the same track as us, or is it travelling down a different track altogether? Does it see a future for itself as a richer and more powerful member of the established global order, or does it plan to go its own way and play by its own rules, overturning the global order as it does so?

The optimistic view is that, throughout history, countries have developed in stages. The idea of externally assisted big bang development is comparatively recent and has not always proved to be an unequivocal success. In Britain our progress was achieved organically over centuries and was not always smooth. We developed systems that suited our needs and our culture.

The Chinese see their development in these terms. They observe that Britain's rapid economic advancement, caused by the Industrial Revolution, pre-dated our embrace of democracy. Indeed, they note, our model at the time, with power concentrated in the hands of a narrow elite, was not that dissimilar from China today, except it was arguably less meritocratic. Everything will come in time, they imply, but not if the cart is put before the horse. They are paranoid about maintaining order and stability, believing that throwing society open will result not in liberal Western democracy but in near anarchy.

They observe too, tartly, that Western attempts at exporting their own political and economic models, arriving flat-packed for assembly in parts of the world with very different histories and cultures, have often been a failure. Has Iraq today become a western-style liberal democracy, or Afghanistan? How have the countries across Africa that were force-fed British rules and systems fared since independence? Russia, they note, was subjected to big bang political and economic change after the fall of the Soviet Union. The outcome, one is left to conclude, was oligarchy and kleptocracy, not liberal democracy.

These arguments are not without force or substance, and we should avoid being presumptuous that Britain, or the wider West, has a template that can be applied to the development of every nation.

It may be that the best we can hope for is incremental positive progress. Slowly the rule of law and the rights of the individual will take root. This will be driven not by a desire to satisfy or impress Western audiences, but by the realisation that these changes represent a necessary pre-condition for the next stage of Chinese advancement. To have faith in this model you need to essentially believe that China is a much bigger version of Britain 150 years ago, and that we can assist by helping to make the civic catch-up process last much less than 150 years.

But what if that is all a delusion, and China is actually on a different track altogether?

Our rapid economic development was followed by the widespread empowerment of our population through democracy and the wholehearted embrace of a rights-based civic culture, but that does not mean that the former is automatically succeeded by the latter. It is perfectly possible to believe, viewed from the perspective of the Chinese leadership, that the absence of democracy, far from being an impediment to their ambitions for global domination, is in fact a distraction that they would be wise to avoid.

In recent decades we have come to associate economic success with liberal freedoms. We note that the most prosperous countries in the world, and consequently the most powerful, are also the most free. The failure of the Soviet Union appeared to emphatically confirm this theory. And in our thinking we typically go even further, arguing that it is only by setting people free in their everyday lives that we can unlock the creativity and innovation that is essential for wealth creation.

But what if this is not true? Or, more to the point, what if powerful people in China believe it not to be true? What if an alternative model is being incubated, in which economic freedom is granted, but authoritarian political control is retained in perpetuity?

If this is indeed the future they envisage for themselves, the repercussions for us will be enormous. Since the end of the Cold War, all the significant powers have shared our values. We Europeans like to gripe occasionally about the American belief in their own exceptionalism, but the reassuring truth is that America is not really exceptional. Like us, they believe in freedom: freedom of religion, freedom of speech, freedom of the press and freedom of assembly. It is a regrettable fact that these freedoms are increasingly circumscribed in Russia, but across the rest of the G8 – in Britain, Canada, Germany, France, Italy and Japan – they are seen as fundamental and inviolable. What is more, they provide the legal underpinning for the whole of the European Union, which demands their strict observance as a precondition of membership.

But the second biggest power in the world has so far shown little interest in these values. And unless the trajectory of its economic development changes, it will, in total GDP terms at least, soon become the biggest power in the world. What then?

The consequences of the Western liberal democracies losing

their global leadership role are hard to overstate.

It is, when boiled down to essentials, about our ability to impose what we regard as a benign form of global order. It is about our ability, through diplomatic and military means, to assert international law on behalf of the weak and the oppressed. It is about our ability to stand up to tyrants and despots. It is about our ability to prevent ethnic cleansing and genocide; to tackle international terrorism and the spread of violent extremism; and to prevent the proliferation of weapons of mass destruction, with all that means for international peace and stability.

Nor is the task of protecting and projecting liberal values simply about using force. It is about the might of our argument and the power of our example. The beleaguered people of the Philippines had good reason last year to be grateful to the governments and people of the West for coming to their rescue after Typhoon Haiyan when nearer neighbours, most conspicuously China, made comparatively little effort to assist.

The liberal values I treasure include living in a country where people are free from oppression and enforced conformity. I want people to have the vote, even when they vote in a way I disagree with. I want them to enjoy freedom of speech, even when I disagree with what they say. I want people to be able to marry whom they chose, to be open about their sexuality, and to feel free from ethnic or religious persecution. I want disabled people to be valued and disadvantaged people to be supported.

These values are not accepted in large parts of the world. In many countries the law is itself an instrument of persecution. The Government sponsored civil liberties abuses in China are widespread. In 41 out of 53 Commonwealth countries homosexuality remains illegal[31]. Even when the law is opaque, in many parts of world minorities are persecuted whilst the authorities turn a blind eye. Being gay in China, or Christian in large parts of the Middle East, is often not a happy existence.

So I am unsympathetic to the view, prevalent on the British Left, that the relative demise of the West will provide the rest of the world with welcome respite from our values-based cultural imperialism. There are many hundreds of millions of people, right around the world, who live in fear and without freedom, and they look to us for the reassurance of knowing that they are not forgotten and are not alone.

Inevitably our power is being diluted. In practical terms – the imposition of sanctions, for example – that makes it harder for Western liberal powers to maintain the grip necessary to achieve desired policy outcomes. Increasingly, the liberal voice is becoming one of many around the global top table. We are working tirelessly with our allies to broaden the pool of like-minded nations, but the scale of this task should not be underestimated.

The challenge posed by the rise of China to the established order, underpinned by international law and overseen by the international institutions, is not just about fundamental human rights and freedoms. It is also about the rules that govern our trade and other financial interactions.

We have, for example, established a system of patents, designed to reward inventors and encourage innovation. But for the system to work properly, everyone needs to respect the rules. If a country takes the view that observing the rules is not in its interest, or even suspects that the rules themselves are little more than a conspiracy by the West to maintain its pre-eminence, they have no great incentive to go along with the system.

Anxieties abound amongst manufacturers about intellectual

property theft in China. Designs are being copied, after the product has been bought or stolen, with no regard for the established rules. Years of expensive investment in sophisticated product development can be wiped out almost overnight, with bleak consequences for companies and shareholders. This does not just apply to top-secret military equipment – James Dyson, of vacuum cleaner fame, for example, paints a sorry picture of the impact of intellectual property theft on his business.

The calculation by China, although they would not say it so overtly, is that this is necessary in order to accelerate their economic development. They need to get to the same technological point as their global rivals, and they will not achieve that objective if they waste time inventing what has already been invented in the West.

There are, of course, grey areas in this debate. At what point does developing the next stage of someone else's invention become a form of plagiarism or outright theft? All humans stand on the shoulders of their predecessors. The makers of American and German cars are indebted to the original inventor of the wheel, but they are not constrained by their intellectual debt nor do they feel obliged to apologise for its appropriation. The Chinese point out that they invented paper, and the benefits to mankind have been felt far and wide.

But we should not get hung up on what are essentially debating points and risk losing sight of the main point. The question remains, is everyone in the world at different points along the same track, making the same journey, with a shared destination – or are we on different tracks, making different journeys, with hardly any shared values-based objectives?

If it is the former, the global economic revolution will continue to change our lives profoundly, but, so long as we take the necessary steps to prepare and adapt, these changes should, for the most part, prove benign.

But if the latter scenario comes to pass, with all that means for the painstakingly devised rules that govern international economic and political interactions, well, that is some prospect to contemplate.

Chapter three
The implications for us

Here is the stark truth: everything is up for grabs; nearly all of our existing assumptions will need to change. Our default mode has become risk averse, with the onus on those who seek change to make their case. This will need to be reversed.

Britain has no absolute right to be more prosperous and powerful than other countries. Just because that has been the case in the past, does not mean it will be the case in the future. We will be rewarded if we make wise decisions. Some of these will be difficult in the short-term, and there will be a huge temptation to put them off or duck them altogether. But the consequences of plunging our heads into the sand will be severe. We need to adapt and change if we are to prosper. Avoiding tough decisions carries as much risk as making bad decisions. If we refuse to confront the scale of the challenge before us, we will suffer the consequences.

We have become used to a settled hierarchy of nations, as have people throughout history because the change in a single lifetime is typically not so dramatic as to be unmissable. But that does not mean that hierarchies do not change: they evolve constantly.

In 1900 Britain was indisputably the most powerful and important country in the world. That is clearly not the case today. Other examples are less obvious but still significant. A century ago Argentina was a major power: today it is the twenty-sixth largest economy[32], and due to consistently disastrous government decision-making, is going in the wrong direction. Argentina is a G20 country, but the position is essentially honorific due to a desire to have a South American nation in addition to Brazil at the new top table of world affairs. Argentina is not a top twenty economy by any criteria. Their biggest objective now should be limited to trying to avoid being overtaken by Colombia as the leading Spanish-speaking South American country.

But the difference between now and the last century is that the pace of change today is faster. Economic integration, powered by instant communications, means the rise and fall of nations can be seen clearly within a working lifetime. The example of South Korea is the object lesson: from poverty to prosperity in just over a generation.

The comforting truth is that, just because one country gets richer, it does not follow that another country gets poorer. Global economic growth is not a zero-sum game: we can all get richer.

But there are two more sobering truths. The first is that vastly different growth rates between the established economies and the fast-rising economies means that we may be getting richer, but our competitors are getting richer faster. Britain, and Europe, will see our GDP rise over the next few decades, but our share of global economic output will shrink sharply. The danger is that small improvements in our absolute wealth will blind us to the damaging implications of our relative decline for our economic, military and political status. Already the recent resumption of modest economic growth risks becoming a convenient excuse to avoid confronting difficult decisions.

The second even more sobering truth is that in the medium-term even the rise in absolute wealth should not be completely taken for granted. Britain today is poorer, in absolute terms, than it was in 2008. Of course the British economy before the crash was artificially inflated beyond its real value, but our measurable GDP at the beginning of 2014 is still lower than it was six years ago[33]. For a population that has become accustomed to continued growth in spending on public services, it has been difficult to adjust to having no extra money to meet these expectations.

What is more, even in the five years before the 2008 crash, the wages of ordinary workers barely grew at all, and actually fell for the lowest earners. The impact on living standards was cushioned by public spending, with £170 billion spent on tax credits between 2003 and 2010[34]; money which is simply not available in an age of enforced austerity. So, for millions of British families, not only have their incomes fallen sharply, but their Government, saddled with debts of £1.3 trillion and rising[35], is no longer in a position to compensate them to the same degree through the welfare system. The result is stagnating living standards, and real wages that are projected to remain at 2003 levels until 2020.

Our situation is now improving. Growth has returned, and Britain's deficit reduction programme is slowly but surely bringing borrowing down. But others remain in a more perilous position and their story should be regarded as a cautionary tale for us. Greece is still trapped in the downward spiral that countries enter when they cannot meet their obligations either by borrowing more money at an affordable level or by raising it through taxation. Governments unable to arrest this decline end up being unable to pay their police, army, teachers and other public servants, who in turn cannot pay their mortgages or bills. On a sub-state level, similar dangers exist in Detroit. Bankrupt countries and cities can be bailed out by others, but real recovery involves painful adjustment and a miserable degree of sacrifice.

In the coming years, some of the established economies will undertake the hard-headed changes that are needed. But some will not. They will succumb to the easy temptation to avoid reform and assume that, because they were successful in the past, they are bound to be successful in the future. That would be a very bad mistake. The new competition will just go straight past them. So Britain must be in the former grouping of countries, willing to pursue the radical reforms that are needed if we are to thrive in an ever more competitive global economy. All of our individual and collective expectations depend on achieving this transition.

So the question for us is not *whether* we make the changes that are required. The only serious question is *how* we make the changes that are required.

I do not pretend to answer this question unfettered by ideological preferences. My contention is that a clear-headed, robust, enlightened and authentic liberalism is not just our best option; it is actually our only option.

It is liberalism's instinctive grasp of both the market economics that drives globalisation and the internationalism that results from it that makes liberalism the only ideology that can navigate us safely through these times. To succeed in the global race we will need a liberal empowerment of the individual, as we seek to encourage innovation and wealth-creation, and meet the needs of an increasingly educated and demanding population. We will also need to make a virtue of enlightened liberal collaboration as we work constructively with other nations to support a rules-based international order.

There are many alternative ideologies being promoted across the Western democracies by politicians of both the Left and the Right who, in different ways and for different reasons, are seeking to turn the tide of globalisation. Nationalists, protectionists, anti-immigrationists, nostalgic conservatives, corporatists, trade unionists, deep-green environmentalists, anti-capitalists – the list is extensive. And they all have their cross-hairs trained on a single enemy: free market liberalism, or "neo-liberalism" as they prefer to call it.

The accelerating pace of global change is unsettling and creates a strong public appetite for implausible alternative political solutions. At a time of financial insecurity, liberalism's opponents do not need to be particularly credible or coherent to garner sufficient support to drag mainstream politicians in their direction. Liberal-minded mainstream politicians face constant demands to stop the world so everyone can get off.

It is important for our future prosperity and security that liberalism prevails, because globalisation can no sooner be resisted than gravity can be defied. It is the great reality and there is no turning back. The question is not *whether* to embrace globalisation, it is *how* to embrace globalisation so as to exploit its opportunities and nullify its threats.

———————

Britain has great strengths and we should play heavily to them: our creativity, our inventiveness, our willingness to innovate, our capacity for unconventional thinking, our generosity of spirit, our respect for a rules-based society, our originality, our subversiveness, and our deep attachment to freedom, choice and individual expression. These characteristics – distinctively liberal, authentically British – will prove to be invaluable in the years ahead.

But we must also face up to our weaknesses, no matter how uncomfortable that process may be. For it is only by understanding what is holding us back that can we move decisively forward. We should be sufficiently humble and self-aware to be willing to contemplate change, because these are also attributes that will mark out the countries with the ability to make a successful transition. I am not talking about minor individual policy flaws, some of which it would be reasonable to consider later: I am talking about deep-seated structural liabilities. We need to identify them and take measures to address them.

———————————

To start with, Britain's class-based social structures and educational outcomes are a barrier to improving our national performance. I want every individual to reach his or her full potential as an end in itself. But as a national objective it is also essential that we maximise the collective value of our so-called human capital.

At present it is all too easy to predict a child's future, by looking at the circumstances into which they were born. To a depressing extent, poor children tend to become poor adults. Disadvantage is passed from generation to generation, paying insufficient heed to ability or effort. As a country, we consequently draw talent from an unnecessarily small pool. This cap on achievement exists in a wide variety of guises. It can be as subtle as whether a person has a feel for the nuances of respectable social behaviour or the right parental contacts to secure a summer holiday internship. It can also take the harder form of dramatically differing formal educational opportunities.

Every mainstream political party claims to want to liberate the innate gifts of everyone in our society. Considering the strength of this consensus, it is highly regrettable, although not wholly surprising, that insufficient progress is being made. That is in part because our politics itself has traditionally reflected class-based interests. But there are also deeper factors in our society that make it difficult for well-intentioned politicians from all parties to affect change, and we need to systematically address them.

Alongside our ossifying class-based social structure, Britain is also constrained by old and overworked physical infrastructure.

It is extraordinary how reliant we remain on structures that were built by the Victorians. The architects, engineers and builders of that era would surely be amazed at how little of their zeal for progress we seem to have inherited and how dependent on their achievements we remain.

Our railway lines, bridges and sewers are, in many cases, heritage exhibits. Victorian homes continue to provide a substantial part of our national housing stock. What-is-more, these 'period' houses from over a century ago are often more in demand from aspirant buyers than many of the houses we are building today. How can we have become less good at building desirable homes than people in the Georgian or Victorian eras?

Even our more recent public infrastructure is now dated. The M25 was the last serious motorway built, and since then we have been mainly tweaking what was first constructed several generations ago. Our main hub airport was designated after the Second World War. There is some progress being made on upgrading our infrastructure, but judged against the fast-emerging powers in Asia, it is not only slow, it is, worse still, painfully lacking in vision.

Our governmental and service-delivery structures were also designed in a different era and are showing their age. It is, for example, a national embarrassment that our upper chamber of parliament is selected from people who have been ejected from the elected chamber, who have failed ever to get elected, who are there by virtue of hereditary succession or by being a bishop, or who have given a large financial donation to a political party. It may seem quaint and harmless to some, but we would find it laughable in any other country. The danger is if it is symptomatic of a national unwillingness to embrace change even when it is manifestly appropriate.

Our system of healthcare was designed after the Second World War when the demands on the service were completely different. Almost seventy years later there are not many other models of service delivery that have not undergone substantial change in order to meet fast evolving requirements.

Our welfare model is even older, designed in an era when fewer women worked, economic migration was rare, life expectancy was lower, and the labour market offered plentiful secure manual jobs. It too has been subjected to endless tweaks and revisions by successive Governments, but as with the health service, there is a resistance to contemplate substantial change.

We see the effects of the global revolution all around us. The way we communicate, the way we work, the holidays we take, the way we shop, how we spend our leisure time – all have been utterly transformed.

In our private lives, and in the private sector, we have adapted to these changes swiftly and impressively. But in the public realm – in our politics and our public services – we seem to lose our collective nerve, giving in to a safety-first hoarding instinct and an impulse to protect. The tragedy is that, in our attempt to preserve the fundamental purpose of our welfare state – the provision of high quality public services available for everyone who needs them – we tend to turn our face against the very reforms that are required to deliver these objectives in the modern age. The ironic result is that those who profess the greatest love for the welfare state are those who, by resisting necessary change, are doing it the most harm.

———————————

Beyond our structures of government and service delivery, there is some reason also to be pessimistic about aspects of our national mood. There is truth in the observation that the Americans have a culture that prizes success whereas we are quicker to be downbeat or sceptical. If you ask an American how they are getting on, they reply "good" or even "great", whereas "fine", "could be worse" or "mustn't grumble" are the standard British responses. I have a deep affection for the British character, but we can sometimes sound suspicious of achievement and cynical about, or even resentful of, aspiration.

I do sometimes detect a loss of a can-do national self-confidence. I was struck, for example, by the level of defeatism that marked the run-up to the London 2012 Olympics. I travelled frequently during this period, and everywhere I went there was an expectation that Britain would host a fantastic Olympics. Only back in Britain was there a relentless and draining negativity about every aspect of the games. It went on and on; a demonstration of national masochism and self-loathing. In the end, unsurprisingly for everyone apart from ourselves, the Olympics were judged a triumph. I do not wish us to be bombastic and self-regarding, but if we do not possess a degree of self-belief as a country, in time, in a more competitive world, others may be inclined to lose belief in us too.

Even in our daily individual lives we seem to have lost some confidence in ourselves. When the Government unnecessarily curtails our freedoms with bans, regulations and centralisation we resign ourselves meekly to our more prescribed and diminished status. Creative individualism is one of our great national assets, but our capacity for energetic and original ideas needs the freedom to thrive.

At the same time, somewhat paradoxically, we are sometimes also seen by the rest of the world as being arrogant and insular. We make little attempt to learn foreign languages. We can convey a sense that it is our role to lecture others and their role to listen to us. We even assume, usually based on scant evidence, that our sports teams should routinely beat their opponents.

All of this adds up to the quirky and hard-to-define collective British character. We are what we are, and there is great virtue in our combination of inventiveness, steadiness and unwillingness to be impressed by charismatic charlatans. My only desire is that we avoid a jaded complacency that assumes, impossibly, both that we will fail and that we do not need to change in order to succeed. That is the worst of all worlds, and is a recipe for decline. We have an obligation to ourselves to realise our national potential.

The final weakness that I wish to identify concerns neither our structures nor our mentality. It is acute and more immediate: the remaining parlous state of our public finances.

We continue to borrow at an unsustainable level. I will deal later with the size of our predicament and the measures necessary to address it. What alarms me in terms of our national mind-set is the limited willingness to accept the full scale of our plight. This sense of denial is a problem across the developed economies, and Britain is better than many others at taking some responsibility for our own circumstances, but we still have a sense of entitlement about being able to receive services that we cannot actually afford.

Our standard of living, including the public services we receive, is a result of our prosperity. There is no right to receive a service that we do not have the money to fund. We either have to accept we will receive fewer services or we have to generate more wealth. Ideally, we would have more efficient public services and a more productive economy. But neither of these will happen automatically. The alternative to confronting these practical choices is to continue to borrow colossal amounts of money from future generations to pour into unreformed and inefficient public services.

———————————

If we show willingness to face up to our deficiencies, the welcome news is that we have numerous national strengths that will stand us in good stead in the global race.

'Brand Britain' has international resonance. The power of the brand lies in its fusion of the historic and the contemporary, the formal and the informal, the deferential and the irreverent. We are the home of the pin-striped civil servant and the Sex Pistols, John Constable and Banksy, the Tower of London and Tate Modern. We can even present the Queen and James Bond, two well-loved global icons, together at the Olympics opening ceremony.

The lure of Britain is not completely tangible and is hard to quantify. Some countries are heavily reliant on their natural resources (Saudi Arabian oil, for example) or their large populations (China). Britain has few natural resources in global terms and less than 1 per cent of the world's population. What Britain does offer is a state of mind; our greatest asset is the natural disposition of our people. It is not a fluke that we pioneered the Industrial Revolution and created the biggest empire the world has ever known. Nor is it entirely down to good fortune that my grandparents' generation helped to save the world from Nazi tyranny. We have, of course, had inglorious episodes and set-backs along the way, but our positive contribution to the development of the modern world has been vastly out of proportion to our size. It is this combination of innovation and resolve that has elevated Britain to a continued role of global significance. From that flow many other advantages.

It is highly beneficial that our language is the global language. It makes us slow to learn other languages, but the pre-eminence of English is a priceless asset. It binds us to the most powerful country in the world. It gives us a head start when we are establishing educational links or business contacts in every continent. English is the language of international communications and the internet.

We benefit too from our time-zone. We are in synch with the still-important European economy and the emerging opportunities in Africa. We are at the cross-roads between North America and Asia. London became a global hub city because it was the capital of the empire. It has retained and enhanced that status because it is a natural global gathering point. That in turn helps to provide the attractions – the financial centre, the theatres, galleries and restaurants – that reinforce the asset.

It is true that America is under-going a 'Pacific Shift', increasingly viewing the world from its west coast rather than its east coast. The shift is significant because it underscores the rising power of Asia, but it is not so absolute that we should conclude that we have been abandoned. There is still a lot of traffic coming through London and our other major cities.

Our elite education is a global attraction. I will turn later to our overall education provision, which is not so competitive, but at the highest level we are still world leaders. Our best universities set international standards for both education and research. Our most prestigious independent schools are highly attractive to the wealthy new Asian elites. Our educational reputation is a lucrative asset for universities and schools that depend increasingly on the income from overseas fees. It also creates a deep and lasting bond between Britain and the thousands of visiting students who later take their place in their own country's business and political elite.

Our high-tech manufacturing is another advantage. It is simply not true to claim Britain does not make anything anymore. We remain a globally significant manufacturing power in quantity terms, producing more cars today, for example, than in the 1970s. But in quality terms we are in an elite league. Last season's Formula 1 champion was a German. His team-mate was an Australian. But the team that produced the dominant car is based in Milton Keynes.

Our success in manufacturing illustrates a wider issue about our labour market in a globalised economy. There are far fewer low-skilled manual jobs than there were fifty years ago. That is a serious problem for people without skills, who need to be equipped to succeed rather than pushed into welfare-sustained invisibility. But it does show that where we can align our national creativity with a well-educated workforce we can be global leaders. Fewer people are employed in high-skilled manufacturing, but they are doing rewarding and highly lucrative jobs which can be sustained in a globalised economy.

Britain's tolerance is also an underestimated international asset. In our country people enjoy not just the opportunity for economic self-expression but for personal self-expression too. We only live once, and while most people want to achieve material well-being in the lifetime, they also want to live free from the dead-weight of enforced social conformity. With the liberal progress of recent decades, we in Britain can easily take the enlightened attitudes of our society for granted. Millions of people elsewhere in the world are not so fortunate. They notice our liberal attitudes and our freedoms and they admire them.

To understand another positive attribute that separates Britain from our competitors, it may be helpful to look at ourselves from an outside perspective. Many Asian countries have an impressively probing and restless urge to analyse which national features contribute to economic success. Finding the winning formulas, then adopting and modifying them, is a route to greater advancement and prosperity. I admire their appetite for self-improvement, and we should learn from it.

A leading Asian politician, visiting Europe to gain a better understanding of the economic and business opportunities, would focus mainly on the three leading nations: Germany, France and Britain. All three are in the top six economies in the world. Germany is the richest and most populous country. But France and Britain are the two significant military powers with the greatest diplomatic reach, in part because they are both permanent members of the United Nations Security Council. All three countries have rich histories and are of obvious intellectual as well as practical interest.

But I would argue that two attributes from amongst these three main European countries should jump out at the curious Asian politician, one very tangible and one rather more elusive.

The tangible asset is the Germans' manufacturing prowess. Germany is the biggest European economy, with impressive living standards, explained in large part by its ability to make and export high-quality goods which are in international demand. As China becomes more affluent, the richest people are now shopping in the global marketplace. They want to buy the best cars, and many of the best cars – Audis, BMWs, Mercedes – are German. Understanding how the Germans design, manufacture and sell their excellent products is a clear roadmap to future prosperity.

The much more elusive attribute is British. It is global thought-leadership.

This point is best illustrated by posing some questions. Which is the most influential global daily newspaper? The *International Herald Tribune* and *Wall Street Journal* deserve honourable mentions, but the winner is pretty clear cut: *The Financial Times*. Which is the most influential global weekly current affairs periodical? This one is in less doubt still: *The Economist*. And which is the most influential global broadcaster? Again, there are serious contenders, CNN and Al-Jazeera perhaps chief among them. But I suspect most people would choose the BBC.

The Financial Times, *The Economist* and the BBC. What do they all have in common, apart from their key role in shaping international political and business opinion? They are all British. It is extraordinary that a country with such a small population should command such disproportionate attention and influence.

We have not arrived at this envious position as a result of a well-executed government plan. If we had, our success would be easier to emulate. But nor has it happened by chance. It has happened because Britain incubates a culture of confident and creative original thinking. The British Government can help to foster this advantage, but it cannot design it.

And that is just a single example. There are many others. At the United Nations Britain is a diplomatic leader. We are seen to have a legitimate role in resolving disputes even when they do not impact directly on us. We do have a global reach and permanent membership of the Security Council, but that is as a result of our leadership qualities, not because of an act of charity by others.

This excellence in thought-leadership is certainly not a result of passing fashion – it is deep-seated. It is seen in our historic ability to design successful democratic and legal systems. It manifests itself in varied and unpredictable ways. People around the world have been kicking balls about for centuries, but someone had to codify the rules of football: eleven players on each team, the dimensions of the goals and the duration of the match. Anyone could have done it, but it was the British who did.

German cars are easy to understand. They are smooth, powerful, with beautiful interiors and doors that make a reassuringly weighty sound when they are closed. Just because they are easy to understand does not make them easy to copy, because they too are a function of a national mind-set, but the manufacturing strength of Germany is still an easily grasped attribute.

Why everyone listens to Britain, even when they do not have to, is a fascinating puzzle.

The last great attribute that deserves its own entry in the ledger of national assets and liabilities is our commitment to playing by the rules. Britain's creative flair needs to rest on solid foundations, and it does, in the form of a rules-based society that has evolved over hundreds of years.

There is widespread international respect for our formal framework of laws. The history of codification, stretching back 800 years to the Magna Carta, provides our system with a weighty gravity. Our legal processes are regarded as fair-minded and honest.

It is easy for British people to take this for granted, but many other countries aim to emulate us. Endemic corruption amongst officialdom and in the legal system blights the prospects of many otherwise promising economies. It is not a coincidence that many of the global financial elite seek to resolve their differences in London's courts. They may not always agree with the outcomes but they recognise that the verdict has been arrived at following a rigorous and impartial legal process.

But it is the culture of respect for the law, rather than just the laws themselves, that is our greatest asset. We may bemoan falling standards, but that is not how Britain is perceived in many parts of the world. We are seen as inherently honest, and remarkably willing to tackle failings when they occur. We are also regarded as being impressively even-handed, with justice applied without favour or discrimination. We award contracts without paying bribes. A Cabinet Minister has gone to prison in this parliament for covering up a minor driving offence that was committed a decade ago. Members of Parliament have had to resign, and some have also gone to prison, for making wrongful expenses claims. We are seen as having an intuitive ability to distinguish between right and wrong, and the resolve to rectify errant behaviour.

I was even struck by the international reaction to the formation of our coalition Government in 2010. Following the indeterminate election result, there were no formal rules dictating what should happen next. Nor was there any real precedent in living memory that could be drawn upon. This could easily have been a recipe for chaos and recriminations. Instead, in a measured and respectful manner, negotiations were concluded, within days rather than months, and a government was formed. Perhaps most impressively, from the perspective of international observers, the opposition parties accepted the legitimacy of the outcome. We take this all for granted too, but many countries in comparable situations have sunk into institutional gridlock, or worse, violence.

Meanwhile, we also benefit from living in a fairly safe country. Last year in England and Wales the murder rate was 1 per 100,000 people[36]. In Brazil it is 22 per 100,000; in Mexico it is 24; and in Colombia it is 33. Even in America it is almost 5 per 100,000[37]. There are countries in Latin America where the rich feel forced to pay for bodyguards to stop their children being kidnapped on the way to school; the calculation being that the protection costs are lower than the ransom demands.

Public respect for political processes and the law, underpinned by a well-functioning legal system, are the bedrock of any successful and prosperous country. Achieving order by consent rather than coercion is fundamental to building a civilised society. And in these respects, Britain is a world leader.

So our strengths as a country are formidable, and our national attributes are widely admired. It would be foolish to write us off. We do have the ability to compete.

Yet these strengths will not, on their own, guarantee success. We also need a clear political plan. That plan, of course, should seek to address our weaknesses and build on our strengths. But more importantly, it should do so in ways that work with, rather than against, the forces of globalisation, and that go with, rather than against, the grain of our national character. It should, in other words, be rooted in an authentic and unambiguous liberalism.

It is often argued that, over the last forty years, the right has won the economic argument in Britain and the left has won the social argument. I disagree. I think that liberalism has won both the economic and the social argument and won them hands down. Indeed, it was only when those on the right set about liberalising our economy, and when those on the left set about liberalising our public services, that a step change in both private and public sector performance occurred.

The lesson, from Margaret Thatcher's privatisation programme and Tony Blair's public service reform programme, was clear: organisations, no matter whether they serve an economic or social purpose, perform better when forced, through competition, to respond to the needs and preferences of their customers or service users. And the people within those organisations perform better when given the freedom and the responsibility to innovate and experiment, whether in pursuit of profit or of social progress.

Add to that the steady advances made in the private sphere to extend people's rights and freedoms, and our national story is one of liberal progress: the spread of economic liberalism, social liberalism and personal liberalism. Indeed, the only area of our lives where liberal progress has been successfully frustrated in recent years has been in our politics. As a result we remain encumbered with the embarrassment of an upper chamber stuffed full of political donors and party place men, and a miserably disempowering electoral system that ensures a majority of MPs need only wear the right coloured rosette to secure their effortless re-election. And we wonder why some politicians can feel sufficiently safe in their jobs to neglect the problems of their electorate, or why so many voters feel disillusioned and disconnected from the political process.

Still, those of us who believe that our democracy would benefit from the same degree of choice, competition and accountability in the political sphere as we routinely demand in the social and economic spheres, must concede that the battle, if not the war, has been lost. In the last four years, the people have been given the chance to adopt an alternative electoral system and declined it. And Parliament was given the chance to democratise the upper chamber and blocked it.

So I will focus instead on the effort to consolidate the liberal gains made in the personal, social and economic aspects of our national life as we seek to get Britain fit for the global race.

Personal liberalism is the celebration of individual freedom and autonomy. It is the allowance of choice for each person without circumscription by the State. It is enthusiastic about genuine diversity and rejects the cloying restrictions imposed by group-think and enforced conformity. It plays strongly to some of Britain's best national attributes: free expression, creativity, originality and the willingness to challenge stale conventional thinking.

A liberal consensus has, for the most part, held sway from the 1960s onwards in Britain, with reforms such as relaxing divorce restrictions, the legalisation of abortion and the introduction of gay marriage all extending personal freedoms and rights. But all three main political parties are prone still to occasional bouts of paternalism, choosing to restrict the exercise of individual freedom

– and with it the need for personal responsibility – in the name of harm or risk reduction.

This is almost always to be regretted, not just for intrinsic reasons, but because our embrace of personal liberalism is one of Britain's great competitive advantages. What, after all, is our key critique of China? Not, surely, that they lack an effective industrial policy, or that they are slothful with their construction programmes. No, it is their disregard for personal freedom and individual choice. The right of every individual to live his or her life as he or she sees fit is a precious, and much envied, characteristic of British life. We chip away at it at our peril.

———————————

Social liberalism is the recognition that the State can empower individuals and help them to realise their full potential. Liberalism has never been about an indiscriminate reduction in the size and reach of the State. More often it is about shaping the State so as to release, rather than suffocate, individual talent.

I believe that the State does have a role in combatting Beveridge's five evils of ignorance, idleness, squalor, want and disease, and that the provision of education, health, housing and employment programmes, together with a proper social security safety net, is a necessary pre-condition for the full realisation of people's potential.

So I am a social liberal, but I would like my own party to do even more to realise the full power of social liberalism. To do so, we must be more than the party of David Lloyd George, or even William Beveridge. We need to be willing to update our thinking, our policies and our service delivery models to equip our population to succeed in the fast changing world of 2014.

Britain's record on social mobility is lamentable. That

the prospects of millions of British children are still so heavily influenced by the circumstances into which they were born is an affront to natural justice. It is a block on our ambition to build a meritocratic and productive economy and an enlightened and harmonious society. Liberal reformers in both the Blair Government and the Coalition have sought to bear down on educational failure, worklessness and welfare dependency – the root causes of inter-generational poverty. But there is much more to do yet. The task now is to accelerate their reforms, not to abandon them.

Countries in the early stages of rapid economic development typically focus disproportionate attention on their elite. That is in part because the decision-makers themselves are self-interested members of the elite, but it is also because it offers a fast-track method for pulling the economy upwards. Their priority is to train a leadership cadre who can then intelligently direct the platoons of workers.

But Britain is in a later stage of development. Every society has people of exceptional talent who should be nurtured and encouraged; it is absurd to be against elitism per se, unless the objective is total equality of outcomes. But our model must be different from the development model in two crucial respects. First, our elite should be able to emerge from anywhere in the population, not just from within the existing elite. And secondly, a successful elite is not enough in a modern economy; everyone has to be equipped to contribute their skills, their ideas and their endeavour.

If we are to succeed in this mission, we cannot take our foot off the accelerator. In our education and welfare systems, we will need more choice, increased competition, sharper accountability, tighter conditionality and further personalised support. If a child is failing at school when he or she could be flourishing, or their parents are languishing on benefits when they could be working, we are failing them and failing ourselves. Britain cannot win the global race in third gear; we needs all of our people to use all of their talent.

The mission for social liberals is to challenge every lazy assumption, every stale orthodoxy, and every special interest that stands in the way of that vision.

Economic liberalism is the belief in free markets and free trade; in competition, choice and wealth creation.

I state these plainly and without embarrassment. For not only is the freedom to create a business and make a profit a key determinant of liberty and prosperity, it is also the essential pre-condition for philanthropy, charity and well-resourced public services.

Yet Liberals, who, let us not forget, differed from the Tories in the nineteenth century because of the hostility of the latter to free trade, have in recent decades become squeamish about evangelising for the benefits of economic liberalism, fearing it will be conflated with uncaring individualism and grasping self-interest.

Yet the enduring truth is that liberalism remains the greatest idea in the history of mankind and economic liberalism the greatest driver of positive change in the world today. Hundreds of millions of people in China and India are being liberated from destitution and squalor. Those countries have different political systems, different cultures and different problems, but they share a key characteristic: they have abandoned inefficient statist economic models and embraced – not entirely, but to a much greater degree – economic liberalism.

The reason there is a global revolution happening today is

because of economic liberalism. It is creating billions of dollars of new prosperity every month. That money is allowing people to achieve standards of living that their parents' generation could hardly have imagined. It is giving people exciting new outlets for their talents and ideas. It is also funding the educational, scientific and technological advances that will take humanity to its next step.

There is a massive danger that Britain – the country that has done so much to nurture and develop the concept of economic liberalism – will lose faith in the most remarkable system of wealth creation in history just at the point when the rest of the world is discovering it.

In the wake of the global financial crash of 2008, politicians in all parties have seemed inhibited about extolling the virtues of liberal economics. We are invited to feel envious, rather than admiring, of those who create wealth, and have become hostile to the very idea of profit. Entrepreneurs who set up businesses that go on to employ hundreds of people often seem tolerated rather than appreciated. Wealth is usually discussed in the context of how it can be taxed rather than how it can be used as capital to fund exciting new business expansions. There is an insidious corporatism spreading into our political discourse which defaults to the presumption that government interference in markets must always be meretricious.

That is not to say that government has no role in the regulation of the economy. It should seek to remove market distortions and barriers to entry. It should facilitate consumer choice, prevent abuses of monopoly power and promote energetic competition. What it should not do is fix prices and wages, pick winners, or, absurdly, categorise businesses based on an official assessment of how effectively they serve an ill-defined wider social interest.

So that is my authentic liberalism: an unqualified, undiluted endorsement of economic, social and personal freedom. In some cases, it requires a less active State, in others, a more active State. These are not new ideas, although they may have new applications. But they do offer the best prospect, indeed the only realistic prospect, for us to prosper in a much more competitive world.

There are two further features of liberalism which will prove invaluable in the years ahead, both of which as much a state of mind as an ideological template. I will label these 'forward not back', and 'outward not inward'. They may sound vacuous, but they capture two sizeable concepts which go to the core of our contemporary political debate.

'Forward not back' is essentially about whether, as we take policy decisions, we do so with our eyes fixed on the horizon, or on the rear-view mirror; whether we have an optimistic or a pessimistic view of the future; whether we think our best days are behind us or are yet to come.

I am proud of many of our historic achievements, but I do believe that we can create a future that is better than the past. That does not mean that I think that all change, in all circumstances, is good. But I do believe a willingness to contemplate change with an open mind is healthy, particularly at a time of enormous and rapid global change.

The powerful instinct at such times is to seek refuge in the certain and the familiar, but it is an instinct we should resist. We cannot know beyond doubt what change will bring, but we can be pretty certain what the result will be if we stand still. We will be left behind; marginalised in the world.

What does 'forward not back' mean in practice?

It means not allowing the welfare state to ossify while society changes around it. The Britain of the post-war period was a very different place from today. The politicians of that era were very radical in their willingness to look to the future. Their mind-set was 'forward not back' and we do not honour their achievements by showing less ambition than they did. If we seek to preserve the post war settlement in aspic, we will succeed only in breaking the social settlement on which it was based, eroding public support in the process.

'Forward not back' means not fetishising preservation over progress in our approach to planning and development. Of course we need to safeguard our natural heritage, but we also have to remember that every house and every road was new once. Young people today want the same things their parents wanted: a home of their own, in a thriving community with good schools and employment opportunities. A block on new housing and infrastructure is a block on the ambitions and aspirations of the next generation.

And 'forward not back' means embracing the industries of the future with the same passion as we lament the loss of the industries of the past. The coal mines were new once; as were the textile factories: they still have a role to play, but they are not where our future prosperity lies. In a hundred years from now we will not be relying on fossil fuels. We know the change will have to be made, and Britain should be at the forefront of new opportunities. When I was at school the internet did not exist. Its full potential is only now starting to be realised as the generation that grew up using it enters the workforce.

So 'forward not back': the confidence to welcome change, to embrace it and to shape it to our own ends.

My other liberal mantra is 'outward not inward'.

There is serious risk that the Western world will respond to the rise of the emerging economies by turning in on itself; that we will devote our energies to building barriers rather than bridges; that we will seek to hoard our existing wealth rather than look to create new wealth.

Many of the Right are anxious about our role in the world. They see change as presenting a threat more than an opportunity, and prefer isolationism as a means of national protection. They rail against the concept of interdependence and are instinctively fearful of any pooling of national sovereignty. When they look outwards to other countries or multinational institutions, they are instinctively drawn towards those, like the Overseas Territories or the Commonwealth, that provide most reassurance from the past.

Many on the Left, meanwhile, rail against the increased inequality that results from global economic integration and specialisation – arguing that the entire system works to the benefit of an internationally mobile elite and to the detriment of ordinary workers. Rather than compete with the emerging economies, they would have us seal ourselves off from them, not, as the Right would have, within a fortified United Kingdom, but within a 'Fortress Europe' with restrictive working practices, gold plated employment rights, industrial subsidies, quotas and trade tariffs.

Globalisation's opponents on the Left and the Right are thus committed to erecting or strengthening barriers to free trade. They just disagree about where those barriers should be placed.

Similar debates are taking place in America, although there the protectionist instinct is stronger on the Left. Like many people, I was inspired by much of Barack Obama's 2008 campaign, but was disappointed by the populism of his claim that he could insulate America's workers from the cold winds of globalisation. It was dispiriting to hear an aspirant leader of a country with pretentions to world leadership tell American employers it was their duty to create "American jobs for American workers".

The authentic liberal view – 'outward not inward' – may not offer the same level of comfort, but it is our overwhelmingly best prospect for future prosperity.

We have no realistic choice but to engage with the world, and embrace globalisation's many opportunities, but we need to have the self-confidence to believe that we can succeed. It is a woefully faint-hearted attitude to think that whenever Britain comes into competition with the rest of the world that we will lose. That has not been true and the past, and need not be true in the future.

Nor is globalisation a zero-sum game. The Left cannot understand that wealth need not be a finite commodity, to be jealously hoarded, but that it is perfectly possible for Britain to benefit from globalisation at the same time as our trading partners also benefit. It is simply not true to believe that the only way to stop British people getting poorer is to stop Chinese people getting richer.

So 'outward not inward': the confidence to shun the illusory comforts of isolation and to realise that active engagement can benefit Britain and the world.

All countries have strengths and weaknesses. Our strengths are formidable and our weaknesses, if we have the resolve to address them seriously, are correctable. If we follow our liberal instincts and traditions; if we build on, rather than chip away at, the economic, social and personal freedoms that are our greatest asset; if we look forward not backwards; if we face outward not inwards; and if we can summon the necessary national self-confidence to embrace globalisation and to shape it to our ends, we will succeed.

Chapter four
Human capital

The events that necessitate the political changes that I believe are necessary are mainly taking place beyond our shores, but the focus of those changes is largely domestic. Globalisation is the unstoppable fact. It is we in Britain who must adapt to it.

In the next five chapters I will describe these changes in greater detail under the following headings: human capital, physical capital, the economy and budget, international relations, and government and the public services.

With the first of these – the raising of our human capital – the task is simply stated: to draw on the full talents and potential of everyone in Britain, for their own benefit, but also because that is the only way we will get our economy to function at full power in the decades to come.

Again, it is worth starting with an honest assessment of our current position.

Here are four broad strengths:

First, we have a supportive civic culture which values original thinking and creativity. It is fairly easy to build the lecture halls, libraries, laboratories and other buildings that make up a university. It is far more difficult to create a dynamic hub for learning, research and collaborative intellectual discovery. Universities and schools do not exist in a vacuum. They may be centres of excellence, but they are still products of their surrounding society.

Britain is a global leader in this area, in large part, I suspect, because of the value we place on individualism and non-conformity. For the time being at least, we boast a civic culture that is more vibrant and imaginative than any of the rising Asian powers. Our creative industries – theatre, film, music, art, comedy – produce a seemingly endless flow of talent that is acclaimed the world over. This is a manifestation of our wider culture; it emerges organically; it is not manufactured by government. As a consequence, it is very difficult to replicate artificially.

Second, our best universities are also of world standard. Some league tables put as many as four British universities in the global top ten; the other six being American. That is a remarkably advantageous position: for educating our own young people, for attracting high calibre international students, and for our ability to attract the minds – and the funds – needed to produce globally significant research.

Oxford and Cambridge are also global brands, built up over

800 years of history, which are difficult to duplicate. After them, the Russell Group universities offer a globally competitive standard of education and research. Our elite students are well served indeed.

Third, our best independent schools are also globally renowned. It is instructive, for example, to visit Dulwich College in Shanghai. It has all the manifestations of an elite British independent school – from house names that celebrate great Victorian figures to cricket matches on expensively cultivated playing fields – but not many of the pupils are British. Many of them are the children of the quasi-stateless global elite for whom British independent schooling is considered the best that money can buy.

Only 7 per cent of British children attend independent schools. For them our elite-level education provides a world class start in life. This is reflected in the disproportionate number of private school alumni at the top of big business, the professions, the civil service, the media and the arts.

And fourth, we have a mass-participation system which provides every child with eleven years of free education as a minimum, and which succeeds in getting hundreds of thousands of young people into university, including the elite institutions, each year. The system has its faults, and is held back by a long tail of failure, particularly amongst the most disadvantaged, but it also has pockets of real excellence, thanks to a good and growing number of inspiring school leaders and teachers. These people are proving every day that nothing is pre-ordained; that deprivation is not the same as destiny; that, by setting high expectations and even higher aspirations, teachers really do have the power to change lives for the better.

Despite the growing number of high-performance state schools, including some in areas of relative social deprivation, the stand-out feature of the British education system is the quality of its elite provision, which rivals anything available elsewhere in the world, America included.

The problem – and it is a very serious problem – is that only a small minority of children benefit from that provision. About 1 per cent of school leavers go on to the globally elite universities, while around 20 per cent (including most of the 7 per cent that are privately schooled) go on to higher achieving universities[38]. Most of the rest go on to less prestigious universities, further education colleges or into the labour market, while 15 per cent are not in education or employment[39]. This closely mirrors the shape of the state school system which, according to the Chief Inspector, is divided between outstanding schools (20 per cent), good schools (58 per cent) and schools that have been judged unsatisfactory or totally inadequate (22 per cent). 250,000 pupils are educated in failing schools[40].

This is the long tail of failure, at the end of a system that even in the middle tends towards the mediocre, that accounts for our relative international decline.

The PISA assessment by the OECD of the comparative attainment of British children makes for grim reading. The most recent tests were sat in 2012 and show the United Kingdom ranked twenty-sixth for maths, twenty-third for reading and twenty-first for science[41].

There are a number of points worth making about these scores. First, our ranking is incompatible in the medium-term with the widely stated ambition to make Britain a successful "knowledge economy". If our people are less knowledgeable than those living in competitor countries then the high-value jobs will migrate away from Britain.

Second, our performance over time has flat-lined at best, and has, in comparative terms, worsened. England's maths score in 2006 was 495; in 2009 it was 493; in 2012 it was 495. Six years of standing still is hugely disappointing, especially when the competition is marching forward. The 2012 tests were the first time Britain failed to make the top twenty in any of the three disciplines.

Third, the fast-rising economic competition, particularly in Asia, is where many of the most outstanding results are being achieved. The Shanghai jurisdiction of China ranked top in every category. Singapore, Hong Kong, South Korea and Japan scored in the top ten in all three academic disciplines. These results offer an insight into the economic future, and underline the stupidity of dismissing the rising Asian powers as "sweatshops" engaged in "the race to the bottom".

Fourth, they highlight the dangers of grade inflation in our domestic exam system. Britain's steep international decline (we were in the top ten in all three categories in 2000) followed by stagnation has happened during the same time period, between 1997 and 2010, that overall GCSE results improved each and every year. I want more children to pass their GCSEs, but I want them to do it because they have achieved a rigorous level of academic attainment, not because the goal posts have been moved to make it easier for them to score.

Fifth, this alarming slip in relative educational performance coincided exactly with dramatic increases in education spending. We are ninth in the international league table on how much money we spend per pupil, but fail to feature in the top twenty by results[42]. The previous Government increased the education budget by £30 billion a year[43], yet Shanghai is beating us comprehensively despite spending far less. I am not saying that there is a correlation between improved performance and spending *less* money. Nor am I saying that none of the increased education spending was valuable – there were classrooms in 1997 that were in need of repair and schools that needed extra investment in IT equipment and books. But I am saying that we should be primarily concerned, in all our public services, by outcomes (the results we achieve) rather than inputs (the money we spend), and should be deeply alarmed when results decline at the same time as spending rises.

Results have started to pick up recently; fewer schools are failing today than three years ago and, overall, Ofsted report that schools improved faster last year than in any other year since the schools inspectorate was formed.

But we still have a mountain to climb. Britain is not performing nearly well enough. We need to ask ourselves some tough questions about why we have slipped into a state of international mediocrity. Our assumptions about what works and how children should be taught need to be radically reassessed.

If the overall outcomes for British children are disappointing, it is even more depressing to shine a spotlight on the performance of those children, predominantly from the poorest families and the most deprived communities, who are least likely to benefit from the elite provision at which Britain excels.

The educational outcomes for children from low income families are a national scandal. We politicians need to ask ourselves how this was allowed to happen in the first place and how, more shockingly, it has been tolerated for as long as it has.

Consider the facts: 41 per cent of pupils still fail to achieve 5 A*-C grade GCSEs including English and maths[44]. This is explained in significant part by the fact that 62 per cent of children poor enough to qualify for free school meals fail to achieve this level[45]. It would be odd if every child passed every exam, but this overall picture of performance is still alarming.

I have a low tolerance threshold for politicians who downplay these failure rates. It is not that hard to get a C grade GCSE. The politicians themselves have almost all reached a reasonable level of educational attainment, and they would not dream of setting their sights so low for their own children. Imagine spending eleven years of your life doing anything and having very little concrete to show for it.

Nor is this most chronic under-achievement confined just to children in schools. The number of NEETs – young people not in education, employment or training – remains stubbornly high. This is a terrible loss of individual potential and an unacceptable drag on our national economic performance.

Meanwhile, there are a large number of children, who are often overlooked, in the middle. Only 7 per cent of children go to independent schools; 18 per cent of children are eligible for and claim free school meals[46]. That leaves a huge block of 75 per cent who are in neither category.

Because of their absolute number, when we focus on the under-performance by Britain in the PISA tables, to a large degree we are looking at these children in the middle, neither highly privileged nor deprived. Typically, they are not among those who leave school with very low, or even no, qualifications. But they deserve just as much attention. For the most part, they are performing much like the schools they attend – not catastrophically, but not brilliantly either, and certainly not as well as they could do, or will need to do, if Britain is to prosper in the years to come.

My experience is that these children are let down in much more subtle and hard-to-measure ways than the seriously disengaged minority whose prospects are blighted by truancy and dysfunctional family support. The pressure on teachers to get children over the C/D line has rewarded the attainment of consistent adequacy rather than excellence. For some children a C grade in a subject will be the limit of their realistic achievement, and the school will deserve credit for helping them get to this point. But for many children a C grade is below what they are capable of achieving. Rather than lifting them to this level, then declaring the job done, schools should be stretching them to achieve higher grades, and the Government is right to be addressing this problem.

Children who excel at primary school, and are given more difficult work to keep them interested and further their development, often find themselves treading water when they move into secondary school. Shockingly, around one in five pupils who gain top scores in English and maths at the age of 11 currently fail to go on to gain any A* or A grades in GCSEs at the end of secondary education[47]. Many of teachers, it seems, are simply unable to fulfil the needs of the brightest pupils, who are forced instead to move at the pace of the average, if not the slowest, pupil in the class. They are the victims of what the Chief Inspector of Schools calls the "curse" of mixed ability teaching.

Any politician who claims an attachment to advancing social mobility should be outraged by the fact that parental income and parental qualifications are a better guide to whether a child will succeed at school than that child's innate ability.

There are multiple suppressants of social mobility for children from low income families, most of them beyond the reach of schools. But one massive barrier that can be overcome, and is within the power of the State to influence directly without encroaching unreasonably into the domestic arrangements of every family, is the quality of formal education that each child receives while at school.

Yet it is children from the poorest homes who are most likely to attend the lowest achieving schools and most likely to receive the lowest quality education. And those in the middle, who are neither rich nor poor, who are most likely to attend a coasting school and receive what is depressingly regarded as an adequate education. Increasingly, it is only the children with the wealthy, educated and highly competitive parents who succeed in securing a truly excellent education, either in an independent school or in the 20 per cent of state funded schools that are rated as being outstanding.

Clearly, that needs to change.

So what do we need do to deliver the best possible education to the largest possible number of children?

A valuable starting point is to look at the children who prosper and succeed in our system and seek to understand better what advantages they enjoy. If we can replicate these much more widely, ideally for all children, then we should make strong progress.

The most striking observation is that well-educated and wealthy parents exercise, often with considerable ruthlessness and admirable determination, a high degree of parental choice. They are typically unwilling to settle for what the system allocates to them and, by using their contacts, their know-how and their money, secure a place at a school where their child will get the best possible chance of realising his or her full potential.

It is simply not true that we do not have parental choice in the education system. We do for wealthy people, but the less wealthy the parents are, the less choice they enjoy.

Parents who can afford the school fees can choose an independent school for their children. 7 per cent of children attend an independent school, but surveys suggest that 57 per cent of parents would send their children to an independent school if they could afford the fees[48].

For parents who could afford to send their children to an independent school but choose not to, or those with incomes that are substantially above-average but still too low to make a fee-paying school a realistic option, there is the choice of moving within the geographic catchment area of the highest performing local state school. This is not a choice open to most people because the house prices and rents are typically higher in the catchment areas of the best schools. Over time they displace less wealthy people who can only afford to move into less favourable school catchment areas, thus reinforcing the process of social segregation between both communities and schools.

The other technique for exercising parental choice, which has the advantage of being completely free, requiring neither the payment of fees nor a premium for a house in a desirable catchment area, is to find a state school place based on an oblique form of selection. Notionally this option is open to a cross-section of society, based for example on their religious faith (real or imagined), but it is exploited most effectively by the wealthy and well-connected. Research by the Fair Admissions Campaign shows that comprehensive non-faith secondary schools admit 11 per cent more children eligible for free school meals than would be expected in their areas, while comparable Church of England secondary schools admit 10 per cent fewer[49]. This is less an observation about church schools themselves, who often have a highly inclusive ethos, and more an observation about the sharp elbows of the parents who apply to them.

But here is the rub: I am not criticising the instinct of all of these parents to try and secure the best education for their child, nor their zealous use of parental choice. But I do not see why this freedom should be restricted largely to wealthy and well-connected people, who use it to reinforce the barriers to social mobility that I wish to deconstruct. I want all parents to enjoy the liberal freedoms currently exercised by a small and powerful elite.

The extension of the liberal freedom to choose a school for your child needs to be accompanied by the same focus on excellence that we see in more successful education systems abroad; in other words, by more rigour.

I want every child to have a substantial core body of knowledge. That requires a teacher with knowledge to impart it to children without knowledge. This can be done in imaginative and enjoyable ways, but it may not always allow for the children to direct the class, choose the topic, or for other forms of "child-centred learning". Times tables might be boring to learn by rote, but without them children will never be able to unlock more intriguing mathematical puzzles. The basic chronology of historical events may seem dull, but they provide the context for the more interesting analysis that will follow. The most creative and inspiring mathematicians and historians all had to learn their times tables and their dates.

I want every child to be taught in an environment that is conducive to learning. There is nothing reactionary about maintaining discipline in schools. Children are at school to be taught, and if the atmosphere makes it less likely that they will be well taught, then the atmosphere needs to improve. This is all the more important because it is often the less gifted children who fall behind in a chaotic classroom environment and who struggle to catch up. Nor is it reasonable for teachers to be expected to work in an unstructured, or sometimes even threatening, environment.

One of the attractions for parents when considering paying for their child to attend an independent school is the expectation of an orderly learning environment. That should be a minimum expectation in all schools, not a premium service.

I would like the length of the school day to be longer. Most state schools finish in the middle of the afternoon. Extending the school day by two hours would have cost implications, but the cumulative effect of an extra ten hours of formal learning every week would be substantial. The Education Endowment Foundation calculates that increasing the length of the school day or the school year adds on average two months additional progress to a pupils' attainment over the course of a year. In addition, pupils from disadvantaged backgrounds benefit on average by an extra half-a-month's progress on top of this, which suggests that extending school time can be an effective means to improve learning for those pupils most at risk of failure.

The very best musicians and athletes spend hours and hours striving to improve. An extra commitment of time yields dividends. It is striking that children at independent schools spend many more hours undertaking formal study. In the highest achieving Asian countries the children spend many more hours undertaking formal study. As a result, by the time they reach 16 or 18, they know more, even if they are no more able. I want the opportunity to know more to be available to all children.

I would like to see an even greater focus on catch-up classes for children who fall behind. Large numbers of children leave school with only a few C grade GCSEs, but this failure rarely comes as a surprise. Rather, it has often been sign-posted months or years in advance. The stark truth is that in a modern economy there will not be many jobs – and certainly virtually no secure, well paid jobs – for people who, after 11 years of education, have failed to reach the most basic level of academic proficiency. Keeping the lowest achieving children engaged is difficult, but to allow them to sleep walk their way into a life of low or no wages is a dereliction of duty.

I want teachers to be of a high standard and teaching to be a highly valued profession. I support initiatives like 'Teach First' which bring talented new recruits into the state education system. The Sutton Trust, an educational charity, has demonstrated how a pupil can gain 40 per cent more in their learning over the course of a year if given a good rather than a poor teacher, and how these gains are even bigger if the pupil comes from a disadvantaged background[50].

According to this research, if we could bring just the lowest-performing 10 per cent of teachers up to the current average, then, all other things being equal, Britain would rise to seventh in the world in reading after five years and to third place after ten years, and to twelfth place in maths after five years and fifth place after ten years.

Of course, all other things are not going to be equal, because the competition keeps raising its game, but that strengthens rather than weakens the point. Low performing teachers must not be protected if they are holding children back. Between 2001 and 2011, only 17 of England's 400,000 teachers were judged to be incompetent by the General Teaching Council[51]. If Britain was the world's best performer that would be a source for celebration, but we are not in the top twenty for any subject, so that level of protectionism within the teaching profession is a serious cause for concern.

I want there to be rigour in the exam system. In the first year of GCSEs (1988) 41.9 per cent of the grades awarded were A*-C and just 8.4 per cent were A*/A. By 2011, the high water mark, these respective figures were 69.8 per cent and 23.2 per cent (there has been a small reduction in both since)[52]. If it were true that today's

19-year-olds were almost three times as brilliant, or taught three times as well, as today's 42-year-olds I would be delighted. But longitudinal and international comparisons do not support such a happy conclusion. I recognise that many children work hard and have genuinely reached levels of attainment worthy of the highest grades, but that does not detract from the obvious conclusion that the overall system has been compromised by grade inflation.

It is, of course, comforting to see rising grades, but unless they are product of improved performance, it is a false comfort. It devalues genuine excellence, reduces the reward for endeavour, and creates a dangerous impression that Britain is more competitive than it is in reality.

I want the widespread and intelligent use of streaming and setting in schools. The 11+ division of children into academic and vocational categories was far too crude and only took account of their aptitude at a particular point in time. But mixed-ability teaching can fail to stretch the most talented pupils and also leave the least talented behind, with the result that the children in both categories fall short of reaching their full potential. Setting within a mixed-ability institution allows for children to progress at a pace that matches their aptitude and for children to rise up the sets, or go down them, if their progress accelerates or slows over time. Setting should be a dynamic process, with multiple upwards escalators in a single institution operating at different speeds, and with children being able to switch with a reasonable degree of regularity.

I want schools to be imaginative about their curricula. The need for basic numeracy and literacy is timeless, but other disciplines rise and fall in relevance as the world changes. The importance of children reaching a level of proficiency in IT has increased over the last two decades, just as the importance of learning Asian languages will increase over the next two decades.

I want children to have a rounded education and be well-equipped for adult life, but I do not want this desirable ambition to mask the need to achieve high levels of attainment in core academic disciplines. There are, of course, good arguments for why children should be taught the basics of personal finance or healthy eating, but the main purpose of a school is not to usurp the role of parents or to socially indoctrinate children. The best educated children have a mature understanding of all of these issues but they also achieve excellent grades in core academic subjects like maths and English. We should not settle for lower expectations for other children, even when the lower expectations are borne out of laudable intentions.

All of these characteristics of a rigorous education are in the gift of schools, and are commonplace in the best schools. But there is one further change I would like to see which is not in the gift of either schools or government: the wider cultural value that society attaches to educational attainment. In the most successful Asian countries their high and rising levels of educational attainment are a matter of patriotic national pride. Parents in these countries take a keen interest in the success of their children. The intensity of South Korean parents, or the so-called 'Tiger Mums' across Asia, may be greater than British cultural preferences would allow, but we should beware of thinking that we have nothing to learn from the Asian countries that are outperforming us. It is not reasonable or realistic to expect teachers to shoulder the full burden of the great national necessity of elevating our educational performance. Parents, in particular, need to be both engaged and empowered to take responsibility.

And that brings me back to my other mantra, which sits alongside greater rigour: the authentic liberal virtue of choice.

As I have noted, free choice already exists for the wealthiest people, in multiple different forms, and no mainstream political party is seeking to remove it. My belief is that this same free choice should be extended to everyone else.

The exercise of choice is the greatest method for raising standards. That is why wealthy and powerful people exercise that free choice with such determination. I have frequently heard politicians claim that "Parents don't want choice; they just want a good local school". Yet these same politicians ignore both the fact that there are still too many bad local schools and that, in a rigid centrally planned system in which the number of school places exactly matches the number of pupils, it is quality that is rationed, with places in the worst schools allocated to the poorest pupils.

Ultimately, the only way to raise standards and achieve widespread, even universal, excellence is either by allowing all parents to choose a good school over the bad one, or, where choice is unavoidably constrained by circumstance, by the Government closing a bad school and replacing it with a good one. The second approach – of monitoring standards, intervening when those standards start to slip and replacing the leadership of the school if standards do not recover – is a necessary part of the overall effort to bear down on educational failure. But it is itself a recognition that parental choice remains far too limited, particularly for disadvantaged families who have been least well served by the system.

The positive impact of choice on quality is supported both in practice and in theory. Unresponsive monopoly provision, usually but not necessarily by the State, leads to worse outcomes than providing services based on a competitive response to the exercising of free choice. When I was a child Britain had a state monopoly telephone provider. It provided an equitable service by being completely useless and inefficient for everyone. Waiting six weeks for a new phone to be delivered and installed must seem as ludicrous to today's teenagers as discovering that shoppers in the 1970s had to navigate their way around supermarkets using candles stuck to their trolleys.

Some people will be quick to point out that installing a telephone is not the same as providing an education. That is true. It is much easier, and yet the state monopoly supplier could not even perform that basic task efficiently and effectively. Why should anyone assume that the State would do a better job with the much harder task of providing high quality education?

The same people will also often argue that choice only works in the interests of the middle class, and that relatively disadvantaged groups are bound to lose out, presumably because they are deemed too ill-informed to choose wisely, or too disinterested to choose at all. This is patronising nonsense. The lesson from choice-based systems around the world is that when choice is extended to poorly served or marginalised groups, as happened when the American Charter School movement began to revolutionise the quality of education in neighbourhoods like Harlem, they embrace it with enthusiasm. So much so in the case of New York's African-American community, that school choice is now talked about in the language of civil rights. As indeed it should be.

After all, there can be few more obvious examples of people's rights being abused than a powerful elite exercising a freedom that they deny to others on the grounds that they are incapable of exploiting that freedom to their own advantage.

So I want all parents to enjoy the freedoms that are currently so jealously guarded by the elite. I believe the State has an obligation to ensure that every child has access to a high-quality education, but I do not see any reason why the State should be the provider of the education. The record of the State in providing services is generally poor. We should not lose sight of the objective, which is ensuring that all children, regardless of their circumstances and background, have an education which allows them to reach their full potential. That is the objective that counts – not the maintenance of state monopoly provision.

So I favour making every school a free school. The head teacher, senior staff and governors should have a high degree of discretion about how they manage their school. They should have complete freedom to recruit the staff they feel will help them to raise educational standards, and to remove staff who are not allowing them to achieve this objective. They should have the freedom to pay what they feel they need in order to attract and retain the best teachers. And they should have the freedom to decide what and how to teach their pupils. They should, in other words, enjoy the same freedoms as independent schools.

Many free schools will wish to collaborate in order to spread best practice and achieve financial economies of scale, and this should be encouraged unless it leads to a restriction of parental choice. Raising standards and delivering improved value-for-money benefits children and parents (and taxpayers).

I have not yet heard a convincing argument for excluding for-profit education providers from our state funded school system. So long as they are delivering a high quality service free at the point of use, they should be welcomed with open arms. After all, the licence to run a school in the state funded system is only granted with conditions; if standards fall below an acceptable level, that licence is withdrawn. Surely, in a liberal society, within budget parameters, it should be for parents, not politicians, to choose what arrangements are suitable for the education of their children.

In any case, many aspects of state funded education are

already provided by suppliers that make a profit. That includes exam boards, text book publishers, building contractors repairing the fabric of the classrooms and coach companies transporting children to school. So there is no great principle at stake about profits being made when education providers are paid using public money.

Furthermore, I do not accept that there is something inherently wicked in the motives of a person or an organisation that makes a profit. Profit is a measure of customer satisfaction – it is unpopular organisations that become unprofitable. It also provides high-achieving organisations, delivering an excellent service, with both the incentive and the means to expand, thereby providing the same excellent service to a wider number of people. Many free schools will be run as not-for-profit trusts, but the broadening of excellent service provision should not be dependent on charity and philanthropy alone. What matters, as always, is successful outcomes. If a profit-making company can run an excellent school, to exclude them from making a contribution based on ideological prejudice would be perverse.

The more considered objection to a choice based system is that, in a world of limited public funds – and therefore a limit to the extent to which supply can exceed demand – absolute parental choice is likely to be curtailed to some degree. There comes a point where this might be expected to apply, but we are nowhere near that point yet. Far more could be done to liberalise the market to allow supply to respond to demand. Instead there are innovations like the Minimum Funding Guarantee, which ensure that school budgets remain much the same from one year to the next, which might make life easier for central planners and administrators, but also provides a wholly undesirable degree of financial security to the least effective and most unpopular schools.

Some politicians are comfortable with sticking at a model of state-guided choice, but it seems to me to be a limited ambition. Allowing choice within tight parameters gives an appearance of parental freedom without making it a full reality. The choice exercised by wealthy and powerful parents is not heavily prescribed, and I do not see why it should be for other parents either.

So I would provide vouchers, paid for by the State, to the parents of every child, to be used where they see fit within the state funded sector, with each institution having the free ability to expand (or contract) their capacity in response to parental demand. The vouchers could be weighted to encourage schools to attract pupils from disadvantaged backgrounds (a more dynamic variation of the pupil premium concept). Only once 100 per cent of each school's income is attached to the pupil will there be fully accountable provision with excellence rewarded and failure penalised.

Once choice becomes more meaningful, of course, competition reaches the biting point where it begins to ratchet up standards, as underperforming schools strive to raise their game to attract new pupils, and highly performing schools battle to maintain their reputations and their local market share.

The system would be more dynamic overall, but not unmanageably so. The OECD and the World Bank have both found that school autonomy and choice can improve student performance, when it is accompanied by intelligent systems of accountability. It already exists here too of course, in the independent sector, where schools compete with each other every day.

Once this system beds in, it would also be reasonable to consider how vouchers could be redeemable at all schools, including existing independent schools. Many independent schools, particularly at the cheaper end of the market, would in any case quite rationally choose to replace their fee income entirely with voucher income, effectively moving into the newly liberated state funded sector.

For the more expensive independent schools remaining in the independent sector there would, however, be real issues which would have to be resolved about school autonomy and the implications of topping-up vouchers, and I do not favour a coercive approach. Any system would be likely to feature what many of the best independent schools already do, using some of their fee income or endowments as a cross subsidy to top-up the value of the voucher for pupils from low income families.

But with all state funded schools becoming free schools with complete voucher funding and with all the operational freedoms of independent schools, the historic divide between the two sectors would in any case have been eroded almost to the point of invisibility. It would be an historic liberal achievement to bridge this divide, not, as some socialists once advocated, by restricting school freedom and parental choice, but instead by extending them to all schools and all parents.

Under the overall system I propose, in which schools become truly accountable to parents for the quality of their provision, there would still be a need for an intelligent system of accountability upwards to government. Raw attainment and pupil progress would still need to be monitored and failure exposed. All parents are keen to exercise meaningful choice at the point at which they select a primary and a secondary school for their child; indeed, it is one of the most important choices they will ever make. But no parent ideally wants to exercise that choice again once their child is settled in a school and has built up relationships with other pupils and teachers. That is why real-time monitoring of standards by Ofsted and others will continue to be crucial.

But in a liberalised system in which highly autonomous

schools compete for pupils, it is crucial that the accountability system is based on outcomes, not inputs. It should not matter to government who runs the school, or how it is run. What matters is whether the pupils are fulfilling their academic potential, particularly in core subjects. Inspection should not be a device to micro-meddle, impose stifling uniformity and restrict innovation.

So that is my authentic liberal model for achieving higher educational attainment for all children: a combination of greater rigour and increased free choice, underpinned by an intelligent, outcomes-focused system of accountability. Government has a difficult balance to strike: it should be intolerant of mediocrity and failure, but should not constrain the freedom of teachers and schools to innovate in pursuit of excellence.

To a liberal, these reforms to empower parents and pupils and to liberate teachers and schools, are of intrinsic merit. But they are also crucial to our ability as a country to mobilise the full talents of our people and to succeed in the more competitive global economy we are entering.

For one thing is certain: if we continue to provide meaningful choice and opportunity only to a rich and powerful elite, we will continue our relative decline. Doing nothing, and carrying on as we have for decades, when the competition from around the world is becoming more intense, may feel like a safe policy refuge, but it is actually a recipe for decline and marginalisation. Whatever the merits or otherwise of how schools have been structured across Britain in recent decades, the proof is in the outcomes, and the outcomes are not good enough. That has to change.

The focus of this chapter has been on schools, which almost every person attends for an extended period, but the spirit of liberal freedom should also percolate upwards into the university sector. Britain's universities and colleges are a national strength, but they can improve further.

The number of hours of lectures and tutorials in most universities is very small, especially for arts courses. That was previously generally accepted by students who were expected to be grateful for whatever the State was willing to provide to them for free. The problem was that the volume and intensity of teaching was often inadequate, and that still remains the case in many institutions today. I want students to have the time and space to think freely and imaginatively, but I also want them to have the exposure to formidable academics that allows them to develop their minds to their full potential.

Whatever view one takes of the student tuition fees introduced by Labour, they do have the indisputable merit, which will become more keenly felt over time, of transforming students from being passive recipients of a service to being much more empowered and discerning consumers. That should improve education standards and academic choice for students.

I strongly support the Government's decision to lift the artificial cap on university student numbers. The era of restrictive central planning for universities, when they were treated like nationalised industries and penalised for exceeding admissions targets, is giving way to an era of authentic liberal opportunity for every individual with the academic talent to benefit from a university course. It is not necessary or wise for central government to set an overall target for the number of people attending university – the decision to continue to study, subject to academic suitability, should be in the hands of each individual person.

Universities themselves are also being required to be more imaginative. They are increasingly competing to provide better courses and meet the enhanced expectations of potential students. They are thinking more about their connections with industry and their global appeal to international students. And they are being required to adapt to the changing nature of the global economy and the rise of Asia.

Twenty-five years ago I arrived at Nottingham University as a new student. In 1989 it was necessary to go to Nottingham to attend Nottingham University, but not today. At the beginning of this century Nottingham University opened a new campus in Malaysia. Five years later it opened another campus in China. These are not franchise operations. Nottingham University today has three locations. It is not constrained by its geographic heritage.

The model is flexible: a student doing an engineering degree could spend one year in Britain, one year in China and one year in Malaysia, and receive the same Nottingham University degree as if he or she had never left the East Midlands. It is academically diverse: Nottingham University in Malaysia has a department studying tropical plants and medicines – the climate in Malaysia being more conducive to this research than in Nottingham. It is also socially diverse: a young Pakistani woman, for example, who wishes to study at a British university but live in a predominantly Muslim country, could enrol at the Malaysia campus. Academics switch between the three locations; for a time the Chancellor of the university as a whole was a Chinese academic.

It is an exciting insight into the future, commendably ambitious and innovative, and a paragon for how Britain as a whole should approach the challenge of globalisation.

Chapter five
Physical capital

Airports, roads, railways, ports, sewerage systems, flood defences, power plants, telecommunications networks and housing – these are the physical assets that constitute the vital building blocks of a modern and successful economy.

If people cannot get to work or transport goods and services to market the economy grinds to a standstill. Our wider society also depends on people being able to travel or switch on the light at home. Building and maintaining an effective infrastructure may be a rather functional topic for political debate but it is a prerequisite for Britain being competitive in the new global economy.

In a previous chapter I discussed the state of mind that Britain will need if we are to succeed: 'forward not back', 'outward not inward'. It is this mind-set, or the absence of it, that provides the context for an examination of our national infrastructure position. My intention is not to examine the merits or otherwise of each and every capital project, but to assess whether we are willing to make the choices which are necessary to have world-class infrastructure.

So this chapter is less about whether we should build a road here or a bridge there than whether, as a country, we are looking forward and outward. It is about the need for ambition, vision, leadership and urgency.

At present I fear we are not willing to rise to the challenge set by the rapidly expanding Asian economies. There is little doubt that the Asian countries have an enormous collective determination to modernise their infrastructure to support their economic goals. Anyone visiting the big Asian cities for the first time, particularly in China, will be struck by the scale and speed of the construction work. It is overwhelming and exhilarating to witness. Britain must have felt similar, albeit on a smaller scale, in the late nineteenth century, with the Victorians in overdrive building houses, bridges, aqueducts, tunnels, train stations and the world's first underground network.

The contrast with Britain today is alarming. We are, of course, capable of building dramatic new infrastructure. There have been good recent examples, particularly in London, like the Jubilee Line extension, the Olympic Park and now Crossrail. But there is little sense of a national endeavour to make our country globally competitive. We seem to cling too keenly to the past, embracing a make-do-and-mend caution. Patching-up the crumbling remains of what we already have more often than not seems to be the extent of our ambition. There is a fatalism in our national outlook.

This will have to change if Britain is to realise its potential as a country and be successful. As with other areas of our national renewal, some of the change will be uncomfortable, but the consequences of not changing will prove to be much more painful.

In 2013, a report by the Civil Engineering Contractors Association found that the United Kingdom's GDP could have been 5 per cent higher, on average, every year between 2000 and 2010 if our infrastructure had matched that of other leading economies[53]. That massive shortfall is almost enough to wipe out the current level of structural deficit that rightly absorbs so much government time. It is a serious and dramatic under-performance compared to our national potential.

The same report painted an even starker picture of the future. It concluded that if our national infrastructure is not brought up to the standard of other developed economies, by 2026 this could create an annual loss to our economy of £90 billion.

A government report on anticipated future road congestion, also published in 2013, underlines the enormity of our infrastructure deficiencies even more sharply. Its central forecast for congestion on our strategic road network from 2010 is for an increase by 2030 of 71 per cent and by 2040 of 120 per cent. Its worst case scenario, the high forecast, is for an increase by 2030 of 137 per cent and by 2040 of 256 per cent[54].

In 2013-14, the Global Competitiveness Index ranked the United Kingdom twenty-eighth for "quality of overall infrastructure"[55]. We cannot keep failing to finish in the top twenty, whether the measurement is of the academic attainment of our children or the standard of our infrastructure, and expect to be successful. We need to do better.

No area of infrastructure development better symbolises our national inertia than the debate over a new hub airport for our capital city. It actually goes beyond infrastructure, acting as a metaphor for the combination of defeatism and complacency that characterises too much of our political debate and outlook.

Demand for air travel will continue to increase. This future demand, including its environmental impact, needs to be managed, but it cannot be wished away. Demand for air travel is forecast by the Department of Transport to increase by between 1 per cent and 3 per cent every year up to 2050[56]. That means, even with existing capacity constraints, passenger numbers at United Kingdom airports are set to increase from 219 million passengers in 2011, to 315 million in 2030, and to 445 million in 2050.

In the first forty years of my life (1970-2010), United Kingdom air passenger numbers increased by 185 million. In the next forty years they are set to rise by another 225 million. Heathrow is already operating at capacity, while Gatwick is projected to be at full capacity by the mid-2020s[57]. Doing nothing is not an option.

Much of this air travel demand will be leisure orientated and, especially for short-haul flights, can be substantially met from regional airports. People living near Glasgow or Manchester do not need to go via London for their summer holiday. Bigger airports like Manchester also have a crucial role in the long-haul market, including with business passengers. This takes pressure off South East airports and, more importantly, opens up new business opportunities for companies in other parts of Britain. Successful major economies have several major airports and that should certainly be the model for Britain.

But none of that changes the key and unalterable fact: Britain has one leading global city that is an indisputable international hub. London is a financial, commercial, legal, political and cultural gathering point. By almost any metric, it is the most important city in Europe, and arguably, even when compared to rivals like New York or Shanghai, the world. London may sometimes exert an unhealthy gravitational pull on the rest of the British economy, but it also pulls wealth and power from around the globe into our country.

A global hub city needs a global hub airport.

Heathrow is a case study of Britain's make-do-and-mend attitude to infrastructure development. It simply is not adequate to deal with the demands of serving a leading global city. The shortage of runway capacity means the airport is constantly operating just below breaking point, with services easily prone to extreme disruption. Flights from Heathrow go to a significant number of cities, but not enough. A British businessperson wanting to expand into South America has to travel through other European hub airports to reach major capital cities like Lima and Bogota. Just as importantly, when Peruvian or Colombian business delegations travel to Europe, they are forced to go through the main cities of our economic rivals before they can get to Britain.

Too much of Heathrow is dilapidated. New buildings have improved the in-terminal passenger service, but compared to the gleaming cathedrals of travel in Asia, our national airport feels like an old warehouse held together by gaffer-tape. It is almost an advertisement for national decline, and that is before the first-time visitor experiences the Piccadilly Line.

On my final journey as a Foreign Office Minister in 2012, flying overnight from Hong Kong to Heathrow, the pilot cheerfully informed everyone that, even though the congestion on that occasion was manageable, we would still be stacking above Biggin Hill for a while so British Airways could avoid using up one of its coveted pre-6.00am landing slots. In other words, the decision had been taken to unnecessarily waste the time of every person on the plane. On one level it felt quirkily and endearingly British (although the appetite for that can fade at the end of a long-haul flight); but the signal it sent to any Asian businessperson coming to Britain for the first time was an embarrassment.

The 2010 Skytrax survey ranked Heathrow as the twenty-first airport in the world for the quality of its infrastructure[58]. The highest performers are the major Asian hubs, with Singapore's Changhi Airport repeatedly voted the best in the world for its infrastructure.

Rectifying our London hub airport problem is not a vanity project; it is a necessity. On a practical level, we need to maintain the status of London as a global hub city. It is hugely important for attracting investment into Britain and maintaining our capital city as a hub for international culture, politics and thought leadership.

It would not detract from regional British airports but complement them. Some long-haul flights are commercially viable from Manchester, but others will only be a feasible option if they operate from a main hub airport. Up to 80 per cent of the seats on the Heathrow to Hyderabad route are filled by transfer passengers[59]. Without a major hub, routes like these do not make financial sense, and Britain will lose (in this example) a direct connection to a thriving Indian city.

The capacity constraints at Heathrow mean a new hub for British passengers is being created by default, but it is located in the Netherlands, not in Britain. Amsterdam Schiphol, with its six runways compared to Heathrow's two, serves 27 airports in the United Kingdom. The result is that Britain is exporting jobs and other commercial opportunities across the channel, with no counterbalancing benefits in return. It is not better for British passengers or for the environment for Amsterdam to serve the British market more effectively than London.

Nor is the compromise option of expanding Gatwick and Stansted a viable alternative in the longer-term. We could, and probably should, build a second runway at Gatwick, but even if we did, the airport would still be at full capacity by 2050. Stansted has ample spare capacity, but that is because people do not want to fly there. Which underlines the crucial point about this debate: what matters is not the total number of runways within reasonable proximity of London; it is the total capacity at a single site. That is the benefit of hub airports. Gatwick, Stansted and Luton airports are fine for what is termed 'point-to-point' traffic, but their expansion would do little to increase the hub traffic that is the mainstay of the business travel that supports a globalised economy.

So the practical considerations regarding the most efficient method for transporting people by air all point towards an improved hub airport near London. But this decision is not just a mechanistic matter to be resolved by people with an expertise in transport. It has much wider ramifications about Britain's role in the emerging new world order and our readiness to be competitive. That is why I support a world-class hub airport for London, not despite my liberal views, but because of them.

We have to make a big choice as a country about whether we respond to globalisation by becoming more internationalist or more insular. I want Britain to embrace the opportunities that globalisation provides. I want us to have the self-confidence to believe that we can succeed in a more competitive global economy. I want us to interact with other countries and learn from their perspectives.

I do not believe we should be constrained by geography when we look for new partnerships in the world. I want us to see opportunities for political and cultural relations with Asian countries in the same way as we have done in the past with other European countries. I want students from Asia, Africa and Latin America to see Britain as a great academic centre, and for our young people to look to study and work in those parts of the world where change is happening fastest.

I want our capital city to be not just a national hub but an international hub. I want London to be the greatest city in the world; the embodiment of our liberal values: entrepreneurial, open-minded, creative and free trading. I want that spirit to infuse all parts of our country as we aim to make the successful transition to a place of pre-eminence in the new global order rather than sheltering in the past. I want Britain to be a prosperous, ambitious country that acts as a magnet for the most free-thinking and innovative people and businesses in the world.

It seems remarkable to me that any liberal would wish to cut Britain off from the world; retarding our internationalism by making interaction between people and businesses harder. There are environmental consequences that stem from air travel which will need to be addressed through improvements in aircraft design, but deliberately reducing Britain's interactivity with the rest of the world will not benefit the environment. People will still travel, and, with globalisation accelerating, they will travel further and more often. But they will simply by-pass Britain as they do so. We will have chosen to cut ourselves off, but the business of the world will continue, only with our contribution diminished. For a liberal trading nation with a proud history of global leadership, that would be a tragic mistake.

So I am unequivocally supportive of building a world standard, modern hub airport for London.

Once such an airport has been built, people will wonder what all the fuss was about. There will be no appetite for going back to the dated, congested, inefficient arrangement that exists today. Every major infrastructure project has its detractors before it is built. The M25 was a highly controversial project, but nobody is arguing now that London does not need an orbital motorway.

What is in short supply in Britain is a visionary belief that we can achieve excellence. The major hub airports in Beijing, Shanghai, Hong Kong and Singapore are not only superior to Heathrow; they also demonstrate a capacity for bold thinking. Hong Kong airport is a wonder of modern engineering. It is on land newly acquired from extending into the sea (as is Osaka, another engineering feat) and took less than a decade to build. Nobody is arguing now that Hong Kong should revert back to using its crowded smaller old airport.

London should have a new hub airport on the north Kent coast, with at least four runways, but preferably six. It should connect by high-speed rail to the north of England and France as well as into the centre of London. It should be built to last for the rest of this century, with the capacity to accommodate the higher forecasts for passenger numbers over that period.

Such a scheme would be hugely expensive, but visionary infrastructure projects that last many decades are always more expensive in the short-term than a make-do-and-mend solution designed to kick the problem beyond the tenure of the existing set of politicians. And let us not forget, infrastructure spending is called investment for a reason. Oxford Economics have calculated that a major new hub airport would add £7 billion every year to the United Kingdom economy[60].

What is harder to calculate are the consequences of

not building a modern hub airport. It is easy to take London's international pre-eminence for granted, but it should not be assumed to be permanent. We have to realise that our prosperity and influence will not be gifted to us, they have to be earned. We should not wait until the businesses and international conferences migrate elsewhere before we are awakened from our state of inertia. Britain needs to demonstrate the same can-do mind-set that typifies the Asian countries that are embracing the opportunities of globalisation with enthusiasm.

It is forecast that a new hub airport east of London could open by 2029 – itself a depressingly protracted timescale – but the sooner we start the sooner it will be ready. The only real question in the meantime is whether our existing capacity can serve the needs of London and Britain until 2029 or whether there will also need to be a short-term expansionary solution to increase capacity over the next fifteen years. The best interim option may be to build another runway at Gatwick, which could be done more quickly and cheaply than at Heathrow, and with less disturbance and disruption. That would allow Gatwick to take on more low-budget, short-haul, point-to-point traffic, freeing up additional hub capacity at Heathrow. But this would only provide a stop-gap solution while the new hub airport was built.

Fifteen years is a long time in the modern world. The most dynamic Asian economies have roughly quadrupled in size in the last fifteen years. Embracing the change needed to be successful in the new world may be difficult but avoiding the change will often prove to be more painful still. We do not have time on our side. We need to be visionary, but we also need to be quicker.

A total absence of urgency also characterises our deliberations about road and rail infrastructure. The underlying assumption is normally that change is risky, and protracted deliberation a positive virtue. But actually doing nothing – or even doing the right thing, but painfully slowly – may be riskier still. This is symptomatic of a misplaced but all too common belief that, in an era of global competition, others will wait for us. I would prefer Britain to be at the forefront of global competition accruing the benefits of being ahead. That is especially true in areas where the need for improvement is so obvious and inevitable.

Britain's roads are suffering capacity-overload and the impact on our economic productivity is severe. For each kilometre of motorway there are 113 million passenger vehicles driven nationally per year. This compares with 47 million for Germany, 39 million for France and 36 million for America. Our motorways carry 46 million tonnes of freight per kilometre per year, compared to 18 million for both Germany and France, and 28 million for America[61].

Britain's railways are also struggling to keep up with demand. When I was born in 1970 there were 30 billion passenger kilometres travelled on Britain's railways in that year. Today it is approximately 50 billion. By the end of the next decade it is forecast to be around 70 billion. Our railways are carrying more passengers than at any time in the past sixty years on a network roughly two-thirds of its size in 1950[62].

Britain's population, according to the Office of National Statistics, is forecast to increase by about ten million to 73 million by 2035. These extra numbers, combined with an increased propensity to travel across the whole population, means that, over the next twenty years, passenger numbers on our roads are forecast to increase by 30 per cent, train passengers by 50 per cent and flights originating from the United Kingdom by 75 per cent. By 2030 the average person is expected to drive an extra 1,100 kilometres a year, make greater use of long-distance trains and take one more flight than he or she does today[63].

The conclusion is surely that Britain not only needs imaginative new solutions, but needs them sooner rather than later. Our situation is already desperate when set against comparable countries like Germany and France. And these are not projections stretching into the next century; they are running through to the end of the next decade and require a response from us now.

The new competition in most of Asia is behind Europe on general infrastructure development because, Japan aside, they started virtually from scratch just twenty years ago. But they are catching up fast. China is building 82 new airports between 2011 and 2015 and their high speed rail network represents the largest infrastructure project in history.

The legacy of under-investment in British infrastructure is already being felt. Since the major motorway building programme came to an end in the late 1970s, investment in Britain's road network has declined sharply in real terms. By 2000, despite the economy enjoying sustained growth, road spending had fallen to 50 per cent of the 1975 level. It has since increased to 75 per cent of the 1975 level. Rail investment declined sharply in the early 1980s to just 25 per cent of its 1970 level, although it has also since increased[64].

So we are struggling with the consequences of historical under-investment and surging demand. McKinsey consultants have estimated that the cost of maintaining, renewing and expanding the United Kingdom's infrastructure will be approximately £350 billion over the next twenty years. That represents a 45 per cent increase on average annual spending since the start of the century.

The Government will inevitably have to spend more on infrastructure. Capital spending does produce a return, and a reasonable transport infrastructure is essential for maximising our economic potential, but there will also be some implications for other areas of government spending. It is simply not feasible to defend every item of current expenditure and at the same time seek to significantly increase the rate of infrastructure investment.

The seemingly endless public inquiries into infrastructure developments, and the bewildering list of arcane additional requirements, add substantial costs and delays to projects. The ritual of planning applications, appeals and counter-appeals is played out over years, or even decades. The assumption again is that there are no economic or social consequences that result from extended delays. That is a false assumption.

To pick one example, the A303, serving much of the south west of England, is a combination of dual-carriageway and single lane trunk road. The congestion at peak times is almost beyond the capacity of any sane human being to endure. The road restricts the freedoms and economic ambitions of people and businesses across Wiltshire, Dorset, Somerset and Devon. The need to dual the length of the A303 (at least as far west as Ilminster) is widely accepted and has been discussed for decades. It is now subject to another review. The total cost of the full upgrade is less than the extra spending commitments for a single year announced at their 2013 party conferences by the two governing parties. Yet somehow, with infrastructure, delay is the default option. The road will have to be dualled at some point, and it is impossible to believe it would take so long in many of our competitor countries. Our inertia seems emblematic of a wider malaise.

Even when there is a broad political consensus on the

need to act the timescales are extraordinarily protracted. HS2 is necessary (although not sufficient) to address our chronic rail capacity problems. It will improve journey times between many of the major cities, but it will also allow for more overall passenger and freight movements. Yet phase one of HS2 is only due to be completed by 2026, by which time the number of passenger journeys is forecast to have risen by almost half as much again compared to today. This process began in earnest in 2012. The distance from London to Birmingham is 140 miles. Is it really only possible to construct ten miles of high-speed track a year? And that is just the first phase. It will not be possible to catch an HS2 train from London to Leeds until 2033.

Opponents of HS2 champion the make-do-and-mend approach to infrastructure, calling instead for upgrades to a Victorian rail network that, ironically, stands as a lasting monument to the visionary can-do spirit of our predecessors. But even the advocates of the project appear to concede already that once HS2 is finished Britain will have done its bit for major railway infrastructure. Our competitors, whether in the established economies or the rapidly emerging ones, are not so timid. We would benefit from better high-speed connections linking all of our major cities across the north, the midlands and west beyond Bristol. We cannot win the global race if we are stuck behind the stopping train.

It is not just transport infrastructure that will need to improve if Britain is to be globally competitive in the decades ahead. Digital communications, energy production, water supply and flood defences all need to operate at an efficient level to support a competitive economy.

The systems that ensure we enjoy clean and reliable water

supplies are now in need of constant repair. It is estimated that a third of the water pipes below London are over 150 years old. Unpredictable future climate patterns and an increasing population, particularly in the South East, put an additional pressure on water supply. The Environment Agency predicts that water demand could increase by as much as 35 per cent per household by 2050, but with better conservation demand could actually fall by 15 per cent[65]. There is no alternative to costly and sometimes disruptive water infrastructure renewal. At the same time, the effective management of water, including more efficient household usage, can ease this burden without any loss of output or quality of life.

Around five million properties in the United Kingdom are exposed to at least some level of flood risk. The numbers at significant risk – calculated by the Government to be 560,000 – could more than double to as much as 1,300,000 by 2050[66]. This is a difficult area to forecast, but nobody is predicting a declining risk. Aside from the terrible disruption that flooding causes to people's lives, it is also hugely expensive. The Environment Agency calculated that the total cost of the summer 2007 floods in England was approximately £3 billion[67]. The 2014 floods were of a magnitude and duration that alerted many more people to the scale of the threat. Since 2010, the Environment Agency and local councils have completed 353 flood and coastal erosion schemes, and we should anticipate that the demand for this work will increase.

The enormous task of renewing and reconfiguring our energy generation and distribution systems has become an increasingly urgent task for government. The closure of old generating systems will reduce electricity margins over the next few years, increasing the probability of supply disruption. The Government estimates that replacing and upgrading our electricity generation, transmission and distribution infrastructure will require further capital investment of up to £110 billion by 2020. At the same time, the Government is committed to cutting our carbon emissions by 80 per cent by 2050 and to sourcing 15 per cent of our total energy consumption from renewable sources by 2020[68]. The Government is to be commended for getting to grips with securing our future energy needs, bringing forward new generating capacity, making necessary decisions on new nuclear infrastructure and showing leadership on new renewable energy production. The alternative is to be overly reliant on highly polluting fossil fuels or on imports from unstable or unfriendly regions of the world. The costs of investing in home grown, cleaner and limitless energy sources may be big, but so is the prize: energy independence, sustainability and an energy infrastructure that supports future economic growth.

While the decisions regarding water supplies, flood defences and energy systems are often about maintaining or upgrading existing infrastructure, the effort to develop a globally competitive digital communications infrastructure is about being at the frontier of new wealth creation. New forms of communication are powering a social and economic revolution and there is no sign of the pace of change slowing. In 2012, global mobile data traffic grew by 70 per cent in a single year. At the end of 2013, the number of mobile-connected devices in the world overtook the number of people[69]. By 2017 it is estimated that there will be 1.4 mobile devices per person. The internet economy is already worth £120 billion a year to the United Kingdom[70].

The digital revolution provides an opportunity for Britain to get ahead of the competition. The Government has intervened to substantially extend the reach of superfast broadband to low population density areas. That has contributed to the expectation by Ofcom that there will be near universal availability to British households of next generation fixed and mobile services well before the 2020 target date set by the EU Commission, with 90 per cent of households connected by 2016[71]. The sooner this task is completed the better, but this level of connectivity is already higher than in other major European countries.

It is already striking how many people are running micro-businesses from home, or working part of their week from home. Small businesses increasingly benefit from the flexibility to be based almost anywhere in the country. Britain's traditional strengths in the service sector, creative industries and communications are all reinforced by the growing utility of new technology. In the coming years, the labour market will become even more fluid. There will be fewer people on long-term contracts commuting for decades from Monday to Friday to a major employer. Instead work patterns will be more varied, fitting in with everything from childcare commitments to the requirements of clients in different time zones.

In many ways this is unsettling. A job for life may seem uninspiring to some, but many people value the high level of security it provides. An increasingly atomised labour market, with more business start-ups and short-term contracts, offers many advantages but certainty and security are not among them. The greatest certainty, however, is that Britain will fall behind if we seek to preserve the labour markets of the past, rather than adapting to the labour markets of the future. The revolution in digital communications will be played out on advantageous territory for Britain: flexible labour laws, English speaking, entrepreneurial and inventive. Those countries with the best educated populations, the most democratic governance structures, and the most dynamic and open economies will be best placed to exploit the opportunities of the digital revolution; it is closed, centralised, command-and-control economies and political systems that will struggle. Britain

– equipped with the right digital infrastructure – should thrive.

———————————

The remaining deficiency in Britain's physical capital is a chronic shortage of housing. The pressure on our national housing stock continues to rise remorselessly, caused by a wide range of factors: the rise in life expectancy, immigration and the changing shape of the family being chief among them.

Between 2001 and 2011 the population of the United Kingdom increased by 4.1 million – not far off the total population of Scotland in a single decade. Over the same period the number of people aged over 80 increased by 453,440 and the number of divorced people rose by approximately 800,000. In 2001 there were 61,000 Polish people living in the United Kingdom; in 2011 there were 654,000 (making Poland the second biggest source country for non-UK born UK residents after India). In 1911 one-in-twenty houses was occupied by just a single person; in 2011 it was one-in-four[72].

Combined, these factors are putting upward pressure on house prices as supply fails to keep up with demand. 232,000 new households are formed in the United Kingdom each year; but in 2012-13 the number of new houses built was 107,000[73]. The number of people on the waiting list for social housing in England is 4.5 million[74]. While average earnings have increased by 35 per cent since 2001, private sector rents have risen by 65 per cent[75]. The average age of a first-time buyer without parental assistance has now increased to 37.

The social and economic consequences are enormous. Families live in cramped conditions. Commuters live far from the workplace. It is becoming ever harder for people to move to high growth parts of the country in search of work. Tenants currently spend about half of their disposable income on rent, with this figure expected to rise.

There are mitigating measures that the Government can take to address this situation at the margins. The levels of net migration over the last fifteen years, which peaked at 252,000 in 2010, can be slowed[76]. Under-occupancy in the social and private rental sectors can be reduced. Schemes like 'Help to Buy' need to be used carefully if people are not to take on debts they later cannot service, but if properly regulated do provide help for people seeking to buy their own home. Shared ownership schemes also provide opportunities for people who would not otherwise be able to afford to buy their own home.

But none of these measures will address the fundamental problem: the shortage of supply. I love our countryside, understand the nervousness about safeguarding our natural heritage, and have no desire to see every blade of grass covered in concrete. But again, as a country, we must decide whether our primary instinct is to look backwards to protect the past or look forwards to make the best of the future. And, as with so many choices we face, I strongly believe that we must embrace change if we are to succeed, and that seeking to insulate ourselves from change will only provide a false comfort.

I do not support every housing development in every circumstance. It is clearly better to develop on brownfield sites before greenfield sites – but brownfield sites alone will not be sufficient. It is clearly reasonable to consider, when building new homes, the impact on traffic congestion and public services – but this cannot amount to a catch-all veto on new developments. Every house was new once. Today's political leaders, and the millions of people who own homes, owe it to subsequent generations not to pull the housing ladder up after themselves.

Individual towns and cities are right to avoid a 'free for all' and plan how houses can best be provided in a way that is sympathetic to the existing surroundings. Developers need to be more imaginative about how they build communities, with decent public amenities, rather than just collections of houses. And residents need to remain mindful of the fact that no town has a natural size. All major conurbations are constantly expanding or contracting; the alternative is to deny people the freedom to move to economically buoyant areas, or to leave economically depressed ones.

There is also scope for the Government to be more imaginative. A prescriptive government may conclude that some big leaps – whole new towns – are required, but a more democratic model could at least allow for incentives – financial inducements for existing communities – to encourage more new homes to be built in the areas where the demand is greatest.

The quality of Britain's physical capital is a tangible asset in the global economy. The countries with the best infrastructure will have a huge advantage. They will move their people, goods and services more effectively, reducing inefficiency and waste. In a highly competitive global environment it will be difficult for any country to prosper if it handicaps itself with inadequate infrastructure.

Our current government is commendably alert to our future requirements. The National Infrastructure Plan, published in December 2013, is an important acknowledgement of the scale of the task that confronts our country in the decades ahead. The Government deserves some credit for leading public opinion, but there is still insufficient vision and urgency in our overall national debate. The biggest decisions of all are being deferred (the hub airport) or are painfully protracted (high-speed rail). There is a willingness to confront the dimensions of our housing problem but hesitancy when it comes to applying the necessary remedies.

Meanwhile our biggest competitors, as always, are not hanging around. China is spending a remarkable 8.5 per cent of its GDP on infrastructure[77], compared to Britain's 2.8 per cent[78]. China has some serious catching-up to do, but at these rates of progress, the gap will be closed rapidly. They are now the second largest air travel market in the world, significantly behind America, but the new Chinese airports are an asset for the future, whereas many American airports have not looked futuristic since the 1970s.

China now has the world's largest toll-road network, a country-wide high-speed railway and six of the world's ten busiest container ports. There is also strong policy support for the continuation of a science and technology infrastructure plan that will run from 2012 to 2030. Far from being a "sweatshop" vision, the clear aim is to boost innovation, support science and accelerate projects ranging from engineering to space exploration.

This is the yardstick against which we will be measured. When all the procrastination and dithering are put to one side, we are still left with the challenge of how to ensure that we have a globally competitive economy with the infrastructure necessary to support it. We must not allow our foot-dragging on new infrastructure to hold back our economic potential and become a metaphor for a wider British complacency and inertia in the global race.

Just as the alternative to being old is not being young but being dead, the alternative to embracing the future is not living comfortably in the past but failing in the future.

Chapter six
The economy and budget

B ritain's economic position in 2010 was dire. It is still difficult today. There is no sustainable route to long-term prosperity that does not involve addressing our predicament head-on. It is the historic task that has fallen to this generation of politicians.

The worldwide financial crash of 2008 left many economies across the Western world badly exposed. It is, of course, true that the effects were not only felt in Britain. It was an international crisis, although it was not truly a global crisis. Australia, for example, did not suffer a recession. And some countries whose economies did contract were well placed to weather the storm, having budgeted prudently in the good times. What the 2008 crash did was to identify the weakest and most indebted economies around the world and put them under a blinding spotlight.

Britain's underlying weaknesses were severe. Only a handful of economies, most obviously in southern Europe, were so brutally exposed. Britain's banking sector, which constituted a larger percentage of our total economy than that of our competitors, was inadequately regulated. Household debt was at dangerous levels. House prices were hyper-inflated. And our government was spending money on the extraordinary assumption that this dangerously overheated and over-extended economic model could be sustained indefinitely.

Those politicians who blame all of our economic problems on international factors conveniently overlook the hubristic claim that the cycle of 'boom and bust' in Britain had been consigned to history. Not once did this boast come with a caveat about the health of the sub-prime housing market in America. It was totally unconditional.

Many millions of British people certainly behaved as if they believed it. Homeowners were taking large amounts of equity out of their houses, which had massively increased in value, and using the money to buy high-value items like new cars. That created a sense, certainly for anyone working in a car showroom, that the economy was surging ever upwards, as the Government promised it would continue to do. But this was economic growth built on sand. That car was not purchased with the wealth created by extra productivity. The economy was not growing on the back of either perspiration or inspiration. It was made-up wealth.

That made-up wealth helped to fund a lavish extension of the role of the State. In 1997-98, Labour's first full year in office, the Government spent £323 billion (37.8 per cent of GDP). By 2009-10, their last full year, the Government spent £673 billion (47.0 per cent of GDP)[79]. This expansion – of over 100 per cent in cash terms

– was partially caused by the need to respond to international circumstances, but it was also a result of policy decisions taken before the 2008 crash.

We were living chronically beyond our means. Even when the economy was growing (or appeared to be growing) and tax revenues were increasing, the Government was *still* borrowing extra money every year. We were storing up pain for the day when reality would arrive. And when it hit, it hit with a vengeance: the economy shrunk by a terrifying 7.2 per cent[80] – the most severe contraction in generations. The British economy has still not recovered to peak levels almost six years later.

As a rule, when a government is borrowing more than 5 per cent of GDP, it is in difficult territory. When it is borrowing more than 10 per cent, it is in basket-case territory. By 2009 the British Government was running an annual deficit of 11.5 per cent – the highest level in the European Union apart from Greece[81].

Britain reached the point where the Government was borrowing an extra £430 million every single day[82]. That is a lot of money to be taking from as yet unborn taxpayers. Next year we will still be borrowing about £260 million a day[83]. That represents progress but the level of borrowing is still alarmingly high. Britain cannot be competitive in the world if we cannot show the discipline to live within our means.

The consequences of our extravagance are now being keenly felt. The Government is currently spending almost £1 billion every week just on the interest on our accumulating debt[84]. That is one thousand million pounds, every week, that could be spent on the skills and services we need to succeed in the future, used instead to fund our over-indulgence in the past. We already spend about the same on debt interest as we do on housing, the environment and transport combined. And this bill will keep rising, up from around £50 billion a year now to around £70 billion a year by the end of the next parliament[85]. Far from going "too far, too fast", the Government is discovering just how long it takes to turn the debt tanker around.

Britain's terrible predicament was exposed and magnified by international factors, but it is not true that the Government was powerless to determine our fate. That is both a counsel of despair and an abdication of responsibility. The power to keep spending and borrowing under control, and to make our country economically competitive, does significantly reside with government. Politicians who are happy to claim credit for the delivery of debt-funded goods and services cannot duck responsibility when our creditors come calling, as they eventually always do.

But enough. What matters now is the task of getting our country back on its feet and fit for the global race.

It is worth reminding ourselves why dealing with our borrowing and mending our economy is so important.

If we spend more than we raise in taxation, we have to borrow the shortfall. That means our current spending is being funded by future generations. It also means that both we and they will have to spend money servicing our debts that could be spent on valuable services. And that is the best case scenario; it assumes that we maintain the confidence of our creditors and can borrow at a reasonable rate. The worst case scenario is when a government loses the confidence of its creditors and gets sucked into a debt vortex, where borrowing costs rise and the State cannot secure the funds to pay its public servants, who in turn cannot afford to pay their mortgages and household bills, causing the economy to collapse.

We in Britain are discovering that even carefully calibrated, cautiously managed austerity is painful. But as others have discovered, it is nothing like as painful as national bankruptcy.

Without extra wealth and responsible budgeting, societies, in time, start to fragment. The reason that people in poor countries do not have modern hospitals, good schools and well-maintained roads is not because they do not want them. It is because they cannot afford them. In such societies, the richest insulate themselves, either by emigrating or by segregating themselves from their compatriots and buying in the goods and services that the government cannot provide. The real victims of government financial mismanagement are those who cannot afford to move out or opt out: the elderly, the sick, the poor and the vulnerable who rely the most on the ability of the State and of society to care for them.

What is more, a poorer and diminished Britain would have less scope to care for others and protect our most cherished values. Our ability to fund international development programmes for the most desperate people in the world would be reduced. Our authority to speak up for the victims of oppression, discrimination and tyranny would be weakened. Our ability to protect and project our liberal values would be compromised.

We must take the measures necessary to avoid national decline, both at home and abroad. It is no use just hoping that this fate does not befall us; each country, to a significant degree, has its own destiny in its own hands. The urgent task of making Britain internationally competitive – 'The Global Race' – cannot be the theme of any single political party; it is a national endeavour.

Authentic economic liberalism, with its emphasis on free trade, free markets, enterprise, choice, competition and innovation, provides the template for wealth creation and national success.

It is a miracle to witness how the adoption of these ideas is transforming the economies of Asia and the lives of their people. It is not a coincidence that China and India, having embraced free-market economics to a much greater degree, are seeing their economies surge ahead. Nor is it a fluke that free-market, free-society South Korea is prosperous whilst closed-off, totalitarian North Korea is impoverished and barbaric.

There is a big danger in Britain that, in our rush to lacerate bankers and hedge-fund managers in order to satisfy the public's appetite for retribution, we fall into the trap of believing that capitalism is our problem.

Every competition – in the market place, in politics, in sport – needs rules, and a means of enforcing them. Where the rules were lax, they need to be tightened; where they were transgressed, they need to be enforced. The task is not to rail in general terms against markets, but to address specific market failures, intervening both surgically and sparingly.

To do otherwise – to turn against the very economic system that we in Britain helped to develop, just at the point when its virtues have finally become apparent to so many other governments around the world – would be an act of historic negligence.

Those Western economies that become furred up with high levels of public spending, taxation and debt, and which burden themselves with inflexible employment markets, will find it increasingly difficult to compete as capital and labour become ever more mobile. It is a delusion shared by nostalgic nationalists and romantic social democrats across Europe that we can seal ourselves off from the changes taking place beyond our national or continental borders.

If we are to become more prosperous, we must compete in the global economy, not pretend it does not exist. We need constantly to ask ourselves what would make a business locate its offices or factories in Britain and then we need to have the strongest global offer.

Some of Britain's attractions are not economic – our free society, our arts and culture. In other areas that I have described – the quality of our education performance and the standard of our infrastructure – we need to improve. But none of this will be sufficient unless we also foster a pro-business, pro-enterprise, pro-employment environment.

It is not by accident that over one-and-a-half million extra private sector jobs have been created in Britain since the General Election. Nor is it down to chance that we have much lower levels of unemployment than France and countries in southern Europe. Flexible labour markets allow businesses to respond quickly and efficiently to changes in demand. The alternative – trying to lock in the status-quo – perversely creates the opposite effect to that intended by making it less attractive for companies to recruit new staff. The young people from across Europe who have come to Britain to work have voted with their feet. Those who have remained must take their chances in labour markets which seem almost to have been designed to shut them out. Almost a quarter of Europe's young people are unemployed. In Spain, the figure is 56 per cent.

In this context, the main role for the Government is to remove impediments to jobs being created. So the Government is right to be lifting Employers' National Insurance – a tax on jobs – for companies when they hire young people. That provides a clear incentive for businesses to bring more people into the labour market.

The greatest incentive for people to remain in work is allowing them to keep more of the proceeds of their labour. The Government's flagship policy of raising the personal allowance to £10,000 a year has had a powerful liberating effect on millions of people. Anyone in full-time employment earning the minimum wage will benefit from a £705 annual tax cut from April 2014. This is, first and foremost, valuable extra money for them to spend, but it also fosters a sense of self-reliance and self-worth, rather than the dependency encouraged by aggressively taxing low earners and then recycling their money back to them in benefit payments.

The Government also deserves credit for cutting corporation tax rates to the point where they are now the lowest of the major industrialised G7 countries[86]. That creates a strong incentive for international businesses to locate in Britain and gives those businesses greater scope to invest, expand and generate more jobs.

Lower taxes on jobs, income and businesses all help stimulate the economic growth that is essential for raising living standards and funding decent public services. Yet tax cuts still cost money, at least in the short term, which could otherwise be used to reduce the deficit. If we are to enjoy the economic benefits that flow from having internationally competitive tax rates and, at the same time, are to eliminate the deficit and bring down our dangerously high levels of government debt, we have no option but to ask some tough questions about the appropriate size of the State.

In 2013-14, the British Government spent 43.7 per cent of our GDP – a higher share than at any point during Tony Blair's decade as Prime Minister. That fact should force opposition politicians to reassess their critique of the Government. But it should also unsettle the Government, whose central claim is that the public sector grew too large for the British economy to support, but who will face the electorate with the public sector still consuming a greater share of the economy than it did for most of Labour's time in office.

It is neither feasible nor desirable for the British State to settle at Chinese or Indian levels (24 per cent and 28 per cent of GDP respectively). Nor is it desirable for it to rise to French levels (56 per cent)[87]. Even a significant number of people who voted for Francois Hollande seem now to be suffering from buyer's remorse when confronted with the low growth and high unemployment that his policies have delivered.

The proportion of GDP spent by the state is as much a measurement of the size of the economy as it is the size of the government. There is no perfect level, with prosperity assured on one side of the line and stagnation on the other, and circumstances will also require remedial government intervention.

The goal is to achieve a balance: a lean and efficient state that does not encumber growth but which can still provide both the investment that underpins economic development and protection for those who need it. Our current spending as a proportion of GDP is unsustainably high and we should aim to reach the levels which have been demonstrated in both Britain's recent past, and in comparable countries, to be most effective and eminently achievable.

From 1997 to 2001, when Tony Blair was returned to Downing Street with another massive parliamentary majority, government spending as a proportion of GDP stayed between 34 and 38 per cent[88]. Yet Labour was still able to implement its programme, the stated aim of which was social renewal.

The Australians, meanwhile, also have a government of comparable size to Britain's in Blair's first term. Since the beginning of this century, under Labor and Liberal administrations, the Australian State has ranged from a low of 34.5 per cent of GDP to a high of 37.2 per cent[89]. During that time their economy has continued to grow strongly and their levels of national debt are very low.

It is not an exact science, and flexibility is required to respond to shocks, but there is a broad sweet spot for having a globally competitive economy with strong growth, investment and social outcomes: this level – between about 35 and 38 per cent of GDP – is, in my view, what Britain should aim for in the coming years.

Our government has a compelling story to tell about Britain's nascent economic recovery, even though there is a long way still to go, but there are worrying signs that authentic liberalism is only partially accepted at the heart of Whitehall.

Faced with an opposition leader whose central narrative is about the shortcomings – and occasionally the evils – of markets, both the governing parties have agonised over whether to ridicule or match his ideas, usually before trying to do both while achieving neither. The result is that Britain has a shortage of politicians who are prepared to bang the drum for free markets, or to call the bluff of those who wish constantly to distort them.

Until recently, it would have seemed unnecessary to remind ourselves why politicians should not intervene in complex markets to deliver politically inspired outcomes to a short-term political timetable. Not so today.

Prices are a function of supply and demand; a calibration of risk and reward. As a market adjusts, it does so in response to millions of consumer and producer decisions, each of which reflects the diverse and disparate goals of the decision maker, as well as the changing environment in which those decisions are taken. In theory, there are two methods for making sense of all these factors: a market, and an all-knowing central planner. In reality, the second of these does not actually exist.

Despite this, it seems that the opposition's promise to freeze energy prices has left voters impressed, the media enthralled, and the Government uncertain. On one level this is unsurprising. The public, who prefer cheap energy to expensive energy, assume this is what the policy will deliver, and, by a margin of four to one, declare themselves to be supportive. This excites the media who proclaim the idea to be a "political game changer", and spooks the Government, who worry that the media might be right. What too few politicians are willing to do is point out that the whole idea is completely unworkable, or ask where such a policy might lead.

Why stop with energy prices? Public enthusiasm for price controls on water bills is likely to be just as high. Even in areas like private housing rents, where the market functions with multiple buyers and sellers, there are politicians who favour intervening to distort the price. And if politicians can interfere in markets to make things they approve of cheaper, why not intervene to make things they disapprove of more expensive? A minimum unit price for alcohol perhaps, or a fat tax on fast food and chocolate?

And why stop at prices? Why not intervene to artificially increase earnings? The minimum wage – set independently at a level designed to eradicate exploitative pay without creating a negative employment effect – has been declared too low by anti-poverty campaigners, so opposition politicians have opened up a new front by deciding to support a 'living wage'. The living wage is like the minimum wage, but higher. It sounds superficially unobjectionable, but if made law, it is estimated it would make up to 250,000 workers unemployed, yet this idea too is now supported by leading politicians in all three major parties. What is not being pointed out is that, ultimately, wages reflect productivity. Politicians cannot just declare that everyone will be richer. There are no short cuts.

Unfortunately, our political leaders, either because they believe it or because they are afraid to admit that they do not believe it, have decided not to confront the delusion that the reason wages are not higher and prices lower is because uncaring politicians have failed to raise or reduce them. This may or may not pay short term electoral dividends, but it is no way to prepare the country for the difficult process of adaptation that Britain must go through if we are to prosper in the new world order.

The same timidity underpins the Prime Minister's and Deputy Prime Minister's regular boast that this government has set a higher top rate of tax than existed in all thirteen years of the last Labour government. What is a voter meant to conclude when hearing this argument? That this government is more hostile to wealth creation than its predecessor? If a 40p top rate was high enough for Tony Blair and Gordon Brown (until his last few weeks in office) then it should surely be high enough for David Cameron and Nick Clegg.

There are many strong arguments for a 40p top rate beyond just recent precedence. Our national prosperity is increased by entrepreneurial wealth creation at higher income levels. Labour in office also made the reasonable claim that two rates – 20p and 40p – was a welcome simplification which reduced the incentive to avoid tax and increased the incentive to work. They were right then and the current government should have the self-confidence to say so.

Authentic liberals should also feel uneasy about confiscationary levels of taxation. The 50p rate had, at the heart of the policy, the assumption that an individual had no more claim to his or her private income than did the State. Above the threshold, the money a person earned was co-owned with the Government, in equal proportions. Given that the income was in fact entirely earned by the individual, this represented an alarming incursion by the State into the private realm. My liberal belief that an individual should be protected from the arbitrary power of an over-mighty state is not suspended when that person succeeds in achieving a certain level of income. A 45p rate is less presumptuous, but it is still too high.

At a time of real economic difficulty, the Government's priority has rightly been to cut income tax for people with low and middle rates of pay. It has made commendable progress, but the timing of the cut in the top rate was regrettable, and suggests the Government has a tin ear for the politics of austerity and shared sacrifice. The better approach would have been to bring the top rate back down from 50p to 40p, but with the change only coming into effect when the Government had met its objective of raising the personal allowance to £10,000. If linking the introduction of the former to the completion of the latter had encouraged the Chancellor to raise the allowance even faster, so much the better.

The next ingredient for long-term competitiveness and prosperity is to live within our means – a necessary precondition for keeping borrowing costs low and debt interest payments manageable. It will be hard for any country to run freely in the global race with a dead-weight of debt strapped to its back.

But beyond the calculations about our ability to borrow and service our debts, the challenge of living within our means is also crucial because it challenges us, as a country, to face up to some big and sometimes difficult long-term choices. What should the State do, and what should it cease to do in the years to come? What should be funded from general taxation and what might be better financed through user charges? How can we encourage more women and older people into the labour market so as to reduce our dependency ratio and increase our economic output? All of these questions and others will need to be asked and answered if Britain is to be truly competitive.

And all the while, the Government needs to stick to the thankless and difficult task of eliminating the deficit – a task that will only be half complete by the end of this parliament.

Both the governing parties deserve praise for the discipline and resolve that they have shown in pursuit of this goal. It is easy to declare a theoretical commitment to spending control. It is much harder actually to achieve in the face of daily calls – from the official opposition, the trades unions, the media and all manner of lobbying groups – for more money to be spent.

What would be a terrible let down now would be for the Government to wobble. That is why it was unnerving to witness the Dutch auction of expensive spending pledges between the coalition parties during the 2013 party conferences, with the Conservatives announcing a marriage tax break and the Liberal Democrats announcing a universal entitlement to free school meals. This transmits a disorientating message about the Government's focus on deficit reduction. It is confusing for the public to see child benefit and the education maintenance allowance being cut on the grounds of affordability only for the Government to then announce a couple of lavish new spending commitments.

Considering the size of the deficit reduction task, I am also uncomfortable about the politically driven decision to ring-fence some departmental budgets, the consequences of which are becoming ever more painful with each new spending round.

The Government is spending £730 billion in 2014-15 and is predicting a deficit of £96 billion[90]. At first inspection, the task of bringing that figure down to zero seems sizeable but manageable. But that is before all spending on the NHS, international development, schools, defence procurement, debt interest and guaranteed generous pensions upratings are taken off the table. The deficit, as a proportion of what is left, suddenly looks much more intimidating.

The only way to stick to the plan when such a large proportion of the budget has been protected is to make deeper cuts elsewhere. This can have a big impact on low spending departments like Culture, Media and Sport or the Foreign Office which have been subjected to dramatic percentage cuts without actually yielding much money. It has piled pressure onto medium-spending departments like Justice, the Home Office and Local Government, which have been forced to make significant cuts to legal aid, the police and local services. This approach has also put pressure on the Department of Business, Innovation and Skills, and on the support they can offer to science, to higher and further education and to high-tech companies in the high growth sectors where Britain could lead the world, like advanced manufacturing or renewable energy; the very investments we should be prioritising.

That is not to say that every cut in these non-ring-fenced departments is undesirable. It is entirely possible to achieve improved outcomes with less money, as the police have demonstrated. But there remains, nevertheless, a distorting effect. It should also be possible to achieve greater efficiencies and improved outcomes with less money in the ring-fenced departments. And it is incoherent to argue, as the Government does, that what matters is the inputs in ring-fenced departments (extra NHS spending) but the outcomes in non-ring-fenced departments (crime falling).

As the ring-fenced departments expand and the non-ring-fenced contract, the burden of spending reductions falls exclusively on a smaller and smaller proportion of the overall government. The budgets of some departments might still justifiably grow in the future, even as total government spending is falling. But in the next parliament, every department should be forced to justify every pound it spends. We should not be content to tolerate inefficiencies just because they exist in an area of spending that is politically sensitive.

The most expensive government department, by a big margin, is Work and Pensions. If we are to live within our means, we have to consider how social security spending can be made more affordable – a task that is magnified by intensifying demographic pressures.

Total welfare spending in 2014-15 is forecast to be £214 billion. Of that, £94 billion will be spent on state pensions and pension credits[91]. Spending on the state pension is actually predicted to fall slightly in the short-term but will rise substantially afterwards – from 5.7 per cent to 8.4 per cent of GDP between 2020 and 2060[92].

A comprehensive welfare state is a hallmark of a civilised society. People who are incapacitated or made redundant from work should not be terrorised by the imminent prospect of penury.

As any country's wealth increases, so too does the public demand for a welfare safety net and the ability of the state to provide it. So it is reasonable to expect that the new global competition, particularly in Asia, will increase their welfare provision over the coming decades. Despite this, welfare provision in the West is likely to significantly exceed welfare provision in the emerging economies.

Angela Merkel summed up the European predicament best when she observed that Europe has 7 per cent of the world's population, 23 per cent of the world's economy, but 50 per cent of the world's welfare spending[93]. The even more stark truth is that Europe's proportion of the world's population is declining and ageing, our proportion of the world's economy is also shrinking rapidly, but the trends for our welfare spending are continuing to rise. Many economies across Europe are already in a precarious economic position. It would be a total dereliction of duty for governments to allow their welfare budgets to drift slowly into a state of complete unaffordability.

So any British government, of any political persuasion, is obliged to re-think our welfare provision. We need better welfare, not higher welfare.

It is, in any case, strange to hear some politicians argue that higher welfare bills should be a source of pride. The vast majority of working-age people want to be in work and want to be earning a decent salary. Much (although not all) of the money spent on welfare is incurred when people's lives do not turn out as they would have wished. That is hardly a cause for celebration. It also has less long-term value than money spent on education, or on transport infrastructure, which benefit both the individual and help to make Britain a more competitive and prosperous nation.

Under the last administration, the proportion of people in receipt of state benefits increased even as the economy grew. In 2000-01, when the period of increased spending began in earnest, 43.8 per cent of households received more in benefits than they paid in taxes (almost exactly the same as the 43.1 per cent when Labour had previously left office in 1979)[94]. But by 2010-11, as Labour left office again, this figure had risen to 53.4 per cent of households. This was not entirely due to the 2008 economic crash

– the number had already climbed to 48.8 per cent by 2005-06[95]. But the fact remains, by the time Labour left office, a majority of households were net beneficiaries of, rather than contributors to, the State.

The welfare state has grown to a size that is neither desirable nor affordable. Universal benefits – including sizable transfers of wealth from struggling workers to wealthy retirees – may have been defendable in an age of plenty. They are much harder to justify in an era of austerity.

The more complicated task is to ensure that no one can live a life on benefits when they could be working, while maintaining a safety net to catch each of us if, for whatever reason, we lose our job. Out of work benefits are no longer paid on an unconditional basis, but there remains an on-going need to help people into the labour market. After all, entrenched inter-generational welfare reliance has no redeeming features. It erodes people's self-respect, motivation and ambition. It is associated with a host of social ills, from mental illness to obesity to drug addiction. Parking people on benefits, then leaving them, safely out of sight and out of mind, is the antithesis of a compassionate liberal approach.

So the Government is right to be reforming welfare and incentivising work. It is right to be introducing a single welfare payment – the Universal Credit – that will simplify the system and ensure that work always pays. And it is right to be dramatically reducing the burden of income tax for people on low and middle incomes. All of these steps will help people to be more self-reliant and help Britain get in shape for the global race.

––––––––––––––––

An economically vibrant and efficiently structured Britain will have the core attributes necessary to succeed, but we will need to orientate ourselves towards the new sources of wealth. The world is changing rapidly: it is becoming far more populated and more prosperous. Our opportunities to trade are multiplying fast but we have to seize these opportunities.

The European Union is Britain's biggest market, and it remains hugely important. We should remain as members and attract more inward investment by being the most outward-looking, flexible economy in Europe.

It is not a choice between Europe and the rest of the world: we need to maximise our opportunities in both. Indeed, they complement each other. Our appeal to potential investors from Asia or Latin America is that we have flexible labour markets, the rule of law, speak English and are the sixth biggest economy in the world. But they also see Britain as a gateway into the world's biggest single market, the European Union.

At the same time, the expanding trade opportunities are largely beyond our continent. In 2012 Britain began exporting more to countries outside the European Union than to countries within it, for the first time since we joined the Common Market in the 1970s. 8 per cent of United Kingdom exports in 2013 were to China[96]. We need to continue to grow our trade with Asia, including with much smaller countries like Mongolia, which was the fastest growing economy in the world in 2013[97].

The World Bank calculated that from 2003-09 the number of middle class consumers increased by 50 per cent in Latin America, with the Brazilian middle class contributing more than 40 per cent of this increase. A third of Brazil's 190 million population – the equivalent of the entire population of Britain – is now deemed to be middle class[98]. This has given rise to a consumption boom linked to the increase in purchasing power.

Between 2006 and 2012 retail sales in Brazil grew by 90

per cent[99]. But Britain has not capitalised adequately on this opportunity. In 2010, we had only a 1.8 per cent share of the imports coming into this growing market, compared to 6.5 per cent from Germany and 2.6 per cent from France. America (15.0 per cent) and China (14.9 per cent) lead the way in Brazil[100]. We are increasing the value of our exports, but in 2012 the United Kingdom was still only Brazil's fourteenth biggest trading partner in terms of exports[101]. We need to improve.

The imperative to seize the opportunities provided by globalisation should inform our view on the movement of people as well as goods and services.

Most European Union migrants to Britain are young, ambitious and come here because they want to work hard rather than claim benefits. They are attracted by flexible labour markets and liberal social attitudes which together give them a fair opportunity to get on in life. They are plugging huge labour gaps in Britain's care homes, farms and service industries, as well as in high-skilled jobs like doctors. They are excited by the opportunity to improve their English language skills and experience our dynamic culture.

Immigration does indeed put extra pressure on housing and schools, but migration is also a two-way street. As many British people live abroad as there are foreigners living in Britain. Whole areas of Spain and France have been altered by the influence of large numbers of British immigrants. Our nationals are working in ski chalets in Courchevel and banks in Frankfurt and bars in Ibiza. Beyond the European Union, the prominent role of British people in Singapore, Hong Kong, Shanghai, and in every major city in the world, is instantly identifiable.

The most exciting benefits from globalisation will not come to us if we are too bleakly pessimistic, not just about human nature, but about Britain. We are admired globally; people from every country want to visit us and understand us better, not because they wish us ill but because they like us. They want to trade with us, buy our goods and services, and sell theirs to us. That is not a cause for regret but for celebration.

No country in the world permits unlimited and unregulated immigration and nor should we. Where there are abuses of the rules and our good-will they should not be tolerated. Immigrants to our country should respect our culture and traditions, and Britons living abroad should behave likewise in their host communities.

At the same time, politicians need to be honest with our population about where our national interest truly sits with immigration policy. It is not possible to compete in the global race without being willing to interact with the other competitors.

The route-map towards economic viability broadly applies to every country. If we are educated to a high level, work hard, live within our means, encourage enterprise, discourage dependency, increase trade and spurn instant gratification in favour of long-term investment, there is no reason why Britain cannot prosper. It will require concerted political leadership. There is no quick fix; no magic pill which by-passes all the effort. Creating a lean, fit and healthy economy to compete in the global race requires the same dedication and sustained application as creating a lean, fit and healthy competitor in any other race.

Chapter seven
International relations

U nless events take a very unexpected turn, the big fact of the twenty-first century will be the rise of China specifically and Asia more generally. By common consent this will be 'The Asian Century'.

This is widely understood and accepted but surprisingly little commented upon. The twentieth century was completely dominated by the West. The two World Wars were European in their inception. The dominant ideas at the end of the twentieth century – democracy, capitalism, individual rights and freedoms – were conceived and developed in the West. The biggest economies were the Western economies. Power – first in Europe, then in America – resided in the West. The greatest scientific innovations and cultural trends overwhelmingly came from the West.

So to move from this situation to a recognition today that we are at the start of 'The Asian Century' is to embark on a dramatic journey over a very short space of time. Shifts of power on much smaller scales than this one have, in the past, been accompanied by periods of considerable instability and often violence. Yet on this occasion, so far, the process has been remarkably smooth. It is worth considering why that is the case.

In part, it is because the shift seems so inevitable. The consensus view, rightly in my opinion, is that there is no point trying to prevent the rise of China, India and other Asian countries. It will happen anyway as these countries, with their massive populations, embrace the ideas and the systems that made us prosperous in the last century and which will make them prosperous in this one. Traditional powers, like Britain and France, each with less than 1 per cent of the world's population, and a rapidly shrinking proportion of the world's wealth, see their best interests as being most realistically served by trying to effectively manage the transitional process, not by trying to frustrate it.

Even America seems surprisingly resigned to this historical transfer of power. Their domestic political discourse produces the occasional spasm of indignation, but these are limited and contained. Although America is not viewing this process as a passive bystander, it is not holding out against it either.

Their policy reaction is the 'Pacific Shift', the extent of which is under-appreciated in Britain and the rest of Europe. It is an important strategic foreign policy decision for America, after decades of seeing both its friends and enemies as being across the Atlantic, to re-orientate in the opposite direction. The 'Pacific Shift' can be exaggerated – countries like Britain, France and Germany remain key political, military and economic allies – but it is real.

The most clear-cut manifestation of the 'Pacific Shift' is the re-focusing of the US military. The rise of China has created a demand for a muscular American presence from countries such as the Philippines, Vietnam and even big powers like Japan who feel threatened by their huge, and seemingly more emboldened, neighbour. But it also reflects a change in the American state of mind.

President Obama, born in Hawaii and raised, for a time, in Indonesia, embodies the shift, but he has only accelerated the process, he did not invent it. Even before him, the traditional idea of what an America president should look like – white, Anglo-Saxon, probably protestant, born in New England, culturally European – has come to feel increasingly anachronistic. That remains a strand in America politics and society, but it is no longer the dominant strand. The new America can be seen more clearly on the other side of the country, in an arc from Texas to Washington State. It is more multi-ethnic, more informal, more innovative and, increasingly, more prosperous. Standing in Seattle, an Asian-orientated America does not feel unnatural.

And yet, and yet... despite this seeming pragmatism towards the rise of Asia, it remains to be seen how this shift in power will play out inside America. The belief in American exceptionalism ("God's Country") and greatness is seared very deep into the national psyche. Americans often think, sometimes with justification, that they are the best in the world at anything in the world worth being the best at. If, or rather when, China overtakes America as the world's biggest economy, what it is to be an American may feel rather different. That does not mean that the Americans will react unwisely, but their friends and allies have an important strategic role in working to ensure that America draws on its best instincts as it adjusts to being *a* world power rather than *the* world power.

So the peaceful shift from Western hegemony to 'The Asian Century' has been assisted by a commendable Western maturity and pragmatism, but the transition has also been helped by the policies and attitudes of Asian countries, including China.

There are many aspects of Chinese policy which irritate the West and some that are more serious than that. The irritation includes an unwillingness to abide by rules which the Western countries regard as universal but which China often regards as being devised by the West to protect their own interests. The infringements include ignoring intellectual property rights and the tolerated production of items like counterfeit cigarettes which undermine Western law enforcement.

More serious is an unwillingness even to engage in proper dialogue on human rights and individual freedom.

And while China is less outwardly aggressive than its detractors fear, neither is it as innocently benign and pacifistic as it claims to be. On the upside, China is allowing freedom and democracy to flourish next door in Mongolia when it could retard it, but it is also turning a blind eye to brutality and abject poverty in North Korea when it could do much more to stop it. China's sheer cynicism when assessing its self-interest with regards to North Korea is coldly unnerving. A major obstacle to a united Korea, with people in the north coming to enjoy the health and wealth of those in the south, is Chinese hostility to sharing a border with an enlarged, democratic and pro-American South Korea. It seems unlikely that this would cause China the difficulty it imagines it would, but their position remains crudely inflexible. China has tolerated millions of North Koreans dying of starvation in order to preserve that strategic objective.

The South East Asian countries also find China over-bearing, although they often shy away from expressing their unease too obviously. Nonetheless, the rise of China has helped to drive the development of the ASEAN grouping of the ten South East Asian countries, emerging as the most cohesive supranational block in the world after the European Union, who find some degree of security in collective reinforcement and increased critical mass.

But most worrying of all is the uneasy political relationship between China and Japan. Chinese (and Korean) antipathy towards Japan runs deep and passes from one generation to another. Japan, outnumbered ten-to-one in population terms, overtaken in GDP terms, and with a defensive island-state mentality, feels the chill of falling increasingly under China's shadow.

All of these tensions provide cause for unease. The rise of China is such a massive historical occurrence, and has happened so rapidly, that there is bound to be some friction. But my view is that, rather than always accentuating the undoubted negatives, there is good reason to be pleasantly surprised at how little tension exists, both between China and its neighbours and between China and the West.

It is easy to imagine far worse scenarios, and it is not just Western countries, but China as well, that deserves some credit for avoiding these.

China is inclined to throw its weight around, but if it did not it would be the first big power in history to avoid the temptation. America has a more benign political system, but it still asserts itself internationally. It regularly intervenes militarily across the globe, which China has so far, mercifully, avoided. And its interventions in Central America to protect its national interest are greater than those of China in South East Asia, just as Russia's belligerence around its border represents a greater menace than any example of Chinese muscle flexing.

And it is easy, but mistaken, to take for granted the

formation of the G20. As an institution it is immature, unwieldy, and certainly a less suitable vehicle for actually getting anything done than the G8. But the very existence of the G20 is a success in itself.

Of course there are any number of multilateral meetings without Western participation, including a regular China-Korea-Japan forum and summits of the BRICs, but these are no different to the Summits of the Americas or meetings of the European Union. Ultimately China, and other Asian countries, have sought to establish working arrangements with the West, in a guarded but rarely wholly unconstructive way. There could easily have been rival G8 groupings set up to directly challenge the authority of the American-led West; instead, all of the world's powers, established and emerging, sit around the same G20 table.

From the British perspective, the danger, as in so many other areas of policy, is that we fail to truly appreciate the magnitude of the changes taking place.

In years to come, academics will study the transformation of the world order in the first decades of this century, and will reflect on the reasons why during the transition, some countries swam and other countries sunk. This is the broad sweep of history. If the twentieth century can be boiled down to the decline of the British Empire, two world wars, the Cold War and the rise of America; then the twenty-first century, in so much as we can predict it, will be about the remarkable rise of Asia.

It is in no way to diminish the wickedness and suffering in Syria to note that the civil war in that country is unlikely to have the same impact on global geo-politics in the twenty-first century as the rise of China and the other emerging powers. Even if we were to witness the triumph of a rejuvenated 'Arab Spring' and the marginalisation of Islamic extremism, the consequences would be smaller and more contained. A serious threat would have been defeated, but the global order would remain essentially untouched.

Here in Britain, I fear, we sometimes struggle to see the wood for the trees.

We like to think we are a nation with a global outlook, but is that true? Draw a line from London to Moscow, down to Kabul, across to Rabat in Morocco, and back to London. Apart from an obsession with America (sometimes justified, sometimes not), the overwhelming majority of Britain's foreign policy focus is within the parameters of this box.

It is instructive to keep this box in mind when listening to foreign policy questions in the House of Commons. The topics fit neatly: The European Union, Israel-Palestine, the European Union, Libya, the European Union, Iran, the European Union, Syria, the European Union, Iraq, the European Union, Israel-Palestine, the European Union...

All of these are important, of course they are, but it is a limited world view. It is concerned with perhaps 15 per cent of the world's population. More significantly, our focus is skewed towards the parts of the world where change is happening most slowly, if at all, and where the dominant theme is often regression rather than progression.

Meanwhile the global revolution is taking place. People across Asia, and to some degree Latin America, are transforming their lives and their prospects. Our political debate is extraordinarily neglectful of this phenomenon. We are a European country, and every country is mindful of what is happening in its own near-neighbourhood. But we are also a global country, or at least we should aspire to be, and that means raising our collective sights.

Britain's strategic priority should be to survive and thrive in 'The Asian Century'.

————————————

Some people would question this strategic priority, regarding it as being absurdly grandiose for a small island in the north Atlantic. Is there a danger of Britain getting ideas above its station? Are we being invited to behave as if the sun still shines on the British Empire?

I reject this critique, not for reasons of nationalism or sentimentality, but because it is so woefully unambitious, lacking in self-confidence and morally neutral.

There is a right wing tradition in British foreign policy which is backward-looking: keenest always to protect and resurrect old alliances rather than build new ones. There is nothing inherently wrong with having a foreign policy which draws on the comfortable and the familiar, but it misses opportunities and is inadequate in itself.

And there is a left wing tradition, which views British (and Western) imperialism as the source of virtually all the world's current ills. Wracked with colonial guilt and paralysed by cultural relativism, its proponents reject the use of British power to project our liberal values. This alternative is one-eyed about the past and blind to both our potential and our responsibilities in the future.

These traditions would have us turn either backwards or inwards or both, and in so doing, would have us abandon our chance to shape the new world order for our own benefit, and for the benefit of others.

Fortunately there is also an authentic liberal strand of foreign policy: self-aware but not self-loathing, confident but not complacent, open-minded but hard-headed, reliable with our allies but imaginative in our attitude towards potential new friends.

Above all, it is a tradition rooted in an unshakeable belief in the universal applicability of fundamental rights and freedoms and in a commitment to the emancipation of all mankind.

Britain's active participation in 'The Asian Century' is about our prosperity, of course. But it is more than that. It is about the protection and projection of our values; our liberal values.

Britain should have the self-belief to play an active role on the world stage. Our presence is far more often welcomed than it is resented. In my direct experience as a Minister, what was remarkable was not how much Britain's global influence has declined but how little. We are a treasured ally and an unwanted foe, not primarily because of the threat we carry, but because of the example we set. We are widely regarded as fair-minded, rigorous, aware of our obligations, non-duplicitous and guided by consistent principles.

The triumph of liberal freedom is not guaranteed. There are causes for optimism, but also plenty of reasons to be pessimistic. After all, it is we, the countries of the liberal democratic West, that are in relative decline.

Anyone living in a country without democracy, free speech, a free media, property rights and the rule of law; anyone living under the shadow of social, ethnic or religious discrimination, or the threat of capital punishment and political detention – any of these people have good reason to want an active and energetic British presence in the world.

We are the only G8 country to reach the UN target for international development spending; we have consistently championed the expansion of the European Union to embrace the formerly repressed people of Eastern Europe; we are a constant agitator for human rights and freedom.

If we treasure our own values, we have to promote them. It

is not reasonable to leave this task to others. We need to influence 'The Asian Century' not just for our own benefit but because we need to be strong if we are to protect the weak.

Britain's ambition should not be limited to just existing in 'The Asian Century'; we should be seeking to shape it.

British foreign policy today is multi-dimensional. It must deal with what William Hague calls the "networked world".[102] There is no single relationship or institution which comes close to capturing all of Britain's foreign policy interests. We need to diversify and deepen our alliances.

Our starting point must be the maintenance of an independent and globalised foreign policy. Multilateralism – working with others in formal clubs and informal alliances – is vitally important, but it is not a substitute for having a robust, self-confident national perspective on the rest of the world. We cannot contract out our foreign policy.

We are the sixth biggest economy in the world. We have the fourth biggest defence budget[103]. We have our own commercial interests, which often place us in competition with countries which are otherwise our allies. We are the only country in the world that is a permanent member of the UN Security Council, a member of the European Union and a member of the Commonwealth. We have our own history and our own relationships.

Our fraternal bond with, for example, Australia (an increasingly significant global power) and New Zealand is impossible for any other European country instinctively to understand. I remember attending a Pacific Island Forum in Auckland in 2011 where one of the distinguished guests was José Manuel Barroso, the European Union Commission President. He is a worldly and experienced politician, but he had never visited New Zealand or Australia before. He was made to feel welcome and enjoyed his visit, but at this event he was a guest at a family wedding, not a member of the family. Nor should we trust others with representing the expressed wishes of the residents of the Falkland Islands and Gibraltar.

There is a view that, unless a country is a superpower like America or China, the role of the nation state in international relations is over – that the world can be grouped into a handful of superblocks: China, America and the European Union in tier one perhaps; India, Brazil, the African Union and the ASEAN South East Asian countries in tier two. I think this analysis is too simplistic. Multilateralism may be the best option available, most of the time, for smaller European countries with populations of a few million people, but we need to maintain the option of greater operational flexibility.

So the challenge is not to wind down our bilateral foreign policy relationships, but to recalibrate and invigorate them to better serve Britain in a rapidly changing world.

For the foreseeable future our most important bilateral relationship will be with America and our most important institutional relationship should, in my view, be with the European Union. So we are right to maintain the highest-level independent diplomatic representation in Washington DC and Brussels, and our interests in Paris, Berlin and at the UN in New York remain hugely significant.

These are core pillars of our diplomacy. But 'The Asian Century' – the move from a G8 world to a G20 world – is stretching out our foreign policy interests. There are more poles of influence. Britain's response to this change – William Hague's "network shift"[104] – is one of the most important and shrewd foreign policy developments of recent years.

Despite falling budgets, Britain has been pushing more people and resources into the great emerging powers – China and India – and increasing our presence in the capital cities of other rising nations like Mexico and Indonesia. The money has been found primarily from scaling back our presence in Europe, particularly in subordinate posts, and from savings in London.

This diplomatic refocusing embodies the wider shift that Britain needs to make to succeed in the new global order. We are not abandoning our most tried-and-tested relationships but we are having to look beyond them.

The task is to make this a whole-of-government process, not just a re-structuring of the Foreign Office. In my experience, the emerging powers are enthusiastic about working with Britain. They want to engage with our Business Department on trade and university education, our Home Office on security collaboration and our Environment Ministry on agricultural exports. Significant progress has been made in broadening Britain's relations with the fast-growing new powers and even more progress needs to be made in the future.

The opportunities for trade with the leading Asian, Latin American and African nations are obvious and central to our future prosperity. But our ambitions for these growing relationships should run deeper.

As we look around the G20 table, the natural inclination is to find alliances with countries that seem most like us: English speaking (America, Canada, Australia) or European (France, Germany, Italy). But Britain has the opportunity now to build stronger political relationships with many major emerging powers. This can be done on the basis of shared outlook and mutual understanding, not just as a cold calculation of mutual self-interest.

There is no reason why South Korea or Mexico, for example, cannot become increasingly trusted and reliable allies for Britain. They may not have been at the centre of our diplomatic radar twenty years ago, but they are countries on the up, growing in confidence, and, crucially, are surprisingly like-minded with Britain. Developing these relationships does not require us to perform painful political or ethical contortions, far from it. We share a largely overlapping agenda. There is no reason why South Korea or Mexico cannot match, or exceed, say Italy as a natural G20 ally.

This is the free-thinking mindset that will enable us to make the fullest use of our independent diplomatic presence in a fast evolving world that is rotating more towards these non-traditional powers.

If we are to make a success of these new opportunities we will also need to adjust our state-of-mind.

Our traditional foreign policy status, combined with our remarkable soft power, opens doors across the globe. But when we walk through those doors we have to be careful about taking too many of our old assumptions with us.

We need to be confident about our own values but courteous towards others.

So I was strongly supportive of the Prime Minister meeting the Dalai Lama, not because I have particularly strong views about Buddhism or Tibet, but because our Head of Government, answerable to a House of Commons elected by us, should feel free to meet with whichever spiritual or political leader he sees fit without being intimidated or brow-beaten by a foreign power.

There is an important principle here about what it is to be

an independent nation. Beyond that, it is delusional in any case to believe that, with this example, the Chinese will respond favourably to Britain losing its nerve and kow-towing to its demands. They may give that impression in the short-term, but they will note that, when push comes to shove, we do not even have faith in ourselves. The logical response to such an absence of self-respect is to bank the weakness and, in time, push again, with the precedent for retreat having already been established.

But there is a fine line between standing up for ourselves and being disrespectful, consciously or otherwise, towards others. Some of our attitudes towards Asian countries, in particular, need a refresh.

I was uncomfortable, for example, with David Cameron's approach towards the Sri Lankans at the 2013 Commonwealth meeting. Of course we should be appalled by the atrocities that have taken place in Sri Lanka, but our Head of Government had accepted an invitation to an international gathering of a supposed family of nations and was a guest in another country. I hope the next time we host an international summit in London our guests do not abandon the carefully-organised formal proceedings to go and empathise with dissident republicans in Northern Ireland before returning to London to hold a press conference in which they threaten our government.

We would not behave like this in Western countries. The parallels are inevitably inexact, but I do not recall any European summits in Madrid being deserted by our Head of Government so he or she could go and meet Basque separatists. And we would not dare to behave in this way towards the Chinese. The Sri Lankans and other countries in southern Asia, including those who are unsympathetic towards President Rajapaksa, will remember how we conducted ourselves.

That may well include India, where Britain struggles to find the right tone. The Indians can be too sensitive to often imagined slights, but we do not always make life easy for ourselves. The language we use in our political debate about immigration, even with regards to high-performing Indian students, is often unwelcoming and uncharitable.

This is a proud and vast country that is surging ahead. Within a generation its economy is likely to be the third biggest in the world. Its new wealth is being built on technology, science and innovation. It has a space programme. It is, by a massive margin, the world's largest democracy.

So why, rather than celebrating this remarkable progress, do we always on official visits seek out the most destitute Indian slum for the main photo opportunity? The British politicians and the British media collude, in an unspoken agreement, to portray India in the most socially backwards light. The more wretched or malnourished the people our political leaders meet, the happier we seem to be.

Again, it is hard to imagine the same discourtesy being displayed in reverse. When a world leader visits Britain we want to show off our country in the best light. The itinerary typically includes visits to Buckingham Palace, the City of London, Oxford University and Stratford-on-Avon. How would we feel if our distinguished guest rejected this programme to travel instead to our poorest housing estate and empathise with the residents about the financial and spiritual poverty of their benefit-dependent lives?

We actually know how we would react, from when the UN housing inspector came to Britain in 2013, toured the poorest areas, and proceeded to denounce the barbarity, as she saw it, of the so-called "bedroom tax". The majority of our leaders and newspapers were aghast at her effrontery, discourtesy and disrespect for our political decision-making processes.

And while I admire this government's energy and commitment to developing relations with China and India, I am less convinced by some of our models of engagement.

We load a plane with politicians, businesspeople, journalists and a host of other hangers-on and embark on a three day jamboree around the host country. It is true that government-to-government relations can play a significant role in establishing business links in China, but even so, it is hard to imagine us having an approach towards America, France or Germany that combined such forced jollity and clumsy propositioning.

Our relations with America, France and Germany are woven into our daily calculations. Our politicians consult with them, our businesspeople trade with them, our academics collaborate with them. We do not approach them in a frenzy of whipped-up interest, assume we have 'engaged', and return again two years later when we become concerned that we may have become forgotten.

At every level, the changes in the world require us to challenge our assumptions. We are right to be shifting our diplomats; right to be seeking more trade; right to be looking to attract more students. And, beyond government, our businesspeople are right to be aiming to collaborate with Asian partners, and our media is right, at last, to be taking a marginally greater interest in Asian affairs. But succeeding in the global race is not just about processes and resource allocations. It is about possessing a mindset that understands it and embraces it and puts Britain at the heart of the newly emerging world order.

Maintaining a formidable independent foreign policy is essential, but not sufficient, in the new networked world. It is too simplistic to declare the end of the nation state, but it is also true that to advance our interests to maximum effect we often need to collaborate with other countries, both through informal coalitions and formal multi-national institutions. It is not a choice between going it alone or throwing our lot in with everyone else: we have to use all of the diplomatic tools at our disposal to wield the greatest influence.

I will come to the United Nations, the Commonwealth and NATO – all important institutions to which Britain belongs – but we should start with our most significant and controversial relationship: the European Union.

I believe that, on balance, Britain's interests, particularly our foreign policy interests, are best served by remaining a member of the European Union.

I come to that assessment dispassionately, without any hugely sentimental or theological attachment to the European Union as an institution. Indeed, it has its flaws as an institution that often make reasonable people despair.

The endemic profligacy, symbolised by the absurdity of the travelling circus that is the European Parliament, with its two homes in Brussels and Strasbourg, is all the more galling when we have been forced to embrace austerity at home. The democratic deficit, manifested in a lofty contempt for any popular views – including those expressed in national referendums – that do not conform to the elite consensus, should trouble every liberal. And the excessive grandiosity, evident in everything from the institutional trappings of superpower status to the tendency to micro-interfere in national matters, is an anathema to people, like me, who do not believe in a European superstate which usurps the role of its constituent nation states.

The European Union has also made a recent catastrophic judgement about which it seems to be blithely unapologetic: using the single currency to force the pace of political integration, at terrible economic cost.

I have never been in favour of Britain adopting the Euro. There appeared to me to be one big argument in favour and one big argument against. The argument in favour is that a single market undoubtedly functions more efficiently with a single currency. America would be a messier and less wealthy market if each of the fifty states had their own money. The argument against is that joining a single currency requires a country to relinquish its own monetary policy as well as some degree of discretion over its fiscal policy. That has always struck me as an excessive and unnecessary sacrifice for an economy the size of Britain's. If the way that people vote in a general election has no bearing on key aspects of economic policy that affect their lives, the main plank of democratic accountability has given way.

I accept that the advantages of the single currency could be argued to outweigh the disadvantages if it had just been adopted by a handful of the most advanced European economies. But the failings of the Euro result from a wider problem with the European Union: the belief in the destiny, or the historic inevitability, of a fully-integrated Europe, no matter how divergent the economies of its member states or how enthusiastic its peoples. This type of zealous determinism always unsettles me.

So my support for British membership of the European Union is not blind or unconditional – quite the opposite. The terms of our membership, and the institutional architecture of the European Union as a whole, need serious recalibration.

The idea of "ever closer union" – an always slightly sinister notion of being dragged further into an organisation than the rules at the time actually stated – is surely now redundant. Britain is not seeking to join the Euro, which would be the obvious manifestation of "ever closer union" and cannot therefore any longer claim to want to be "at the heart of Europe".

So the new European Union needs to acknowledge that it will have two rings of membership: an inner ring of countries that use the single currency and embrace the concept of "ever closer union", and an outer ring. And Britain will be in the outer ring. Our task is to define what it means to be the biggest player in the outer ring. We are members of the club, and should be active participants in its workings, but we have no right to dictate or veto policies that are the natural preserve of Eurozone members unless they have a very direct impact on us.

Indeed, in time I would go further and add a third ring of more loosely affiliated members. I do believe it is in Britain and Europe's interests for Turkey not to be frozen out, and for other European countries with large populations, most notably Ukraine, to also come within a formal grouping. But it is not politically or economically realistic for their people to enjoy complete freedom of movement in the European Union, or for their economies to be contorted into the Eurozone. If that is the only option on the table it will be vetoed. So we need a more imaginative solution: less than Turkey and others may like, but more than they would otherwise get.

If we can establish a European Union that reflects the reality of European public opinion today rather than the idealism of the post-war generation, then there is a real basis for Britain to be a positive and constructive member, furthering our own interests, and often those of Europe as a whole.

For a start, there is benefit in the scale – the sheer critical mass – that the European Union provides. It is the largest single market in the world. It has sophisticated social structures, great educational institutions, mature democracies and some of the biggest businesses in the world. Its people, by global standards, are phenomenally wealthy.

It is easy for China to ignore most European countries. It is possible for China to partially ignore Britain, Germany, France and Italy. But it is not really possible to ignore Europe as a whole. That does give us collective muscle, in trade negotiations, for example, or at climate change summits, that individual member states, even big ones like Britain, would not otherwise possess.

The question then is how Britain can turn that scale to our advantage. When it comes to diplomatic force magnification and projection, Britain is typically a leader in the European Union, and often the leader. It is unquestionably in our security interests to prevent Iran from acquiring a nuclear weapon, and to do this with sufficient alacrity that Israel does not feel the need to start a pre-emptive war. The oil sanctions against Iran have bitten hard, but they would not have done so if they had been imposed unilaterally by Britain. They needed the critical mass that the European Union, with British leadership, provides.

This collective weight is also a vital economic advantage. Virtually every country in the world wants to sell its goods and services within the European Union. Britain, by being outward-looking and resisting the protectionist instincts of some other European countries, is ideally placed to use the European Union as a powerful force to drive forward greater global trade, raising prosperity and living standards.

Within the single market our goods, services and people move freely. It is easy to take that for granted now, but it is an enormous asset for British businesses. Of course other European countries would still trade with us if we left the European Union, but it would be considerably harder. The result of removing barriers to free trade, as every liberal knows, is more jobs and more wealth.

We should also not lose sight of the value of the European

Union's critical mass not just in the diplomatic and economic spheres but also in the effort to project our values. There is no continent in the world that has a greater instinctive attachment to human rights. One area of overwhelming consensus in the European Union is the belief in open societies and individual liberty. The world would feel like a less liberal place without the European Union. Indeed, it is the very prospect of membership of the European Union that has been used as a successful lever to promote progress in European countries that have lagged behind in the rights that they afford their citizens.

The assimilation of the countries of Eastern Europe has arguably been the European Union's greatest success. The people of these countries, previously suppressed and relatively financially impoverished, now enjoy democracy, freedom and capitalism, with all the rewards that these bring. The reason for the turmoil in the Ukraine is because many of their population can see the contrast between the liberal emancipation that the European Union offers from the West and the strong arm control that Russia is looking to assert from the East.

It is in this spirit that I also break with the new consensus in British politics that it was a terrible mistake to allow people from new EU states in Eastern Europe, principally Poland, to work in Britain from 2004. I think the economic benefits have been significant, as many employers will testify, but I also see a wider context. Britain held the line against the Soviet Union in the Cold War because we believed all people should benefit from liberal freedoms and be spared from communist oppression. That we were able to achieve that objective and share our success with people in countries like Poland is a genuine historical achievement. We did not tear down the Berlin Wall only to erect a new barrier between the people of Western and Eastern Europe. We should feel some pride that Britain was sufficiently enlightened to seize opportunities for friendship when some other Western European countries were keener on the theory of a non-divided Europe than on the reality.

The final argument for Britain remaining as a member of the European Union is a rather unheroic and pragmatic one: it will still be there if we leave. It will do some things well and some things badly, but it will still wield huge influence and continue to impact on us.

I have attended EU-Asian Summits. They are longer on stodgy formalities than they are on decisive outcomes. But it would feel to me like a dereliction of national duty to walk away from these events, leaving the German Chancellor and the French President to deepen relations with the Chinese Premier and the Indian Prime Minister, with us no longer in the room.

If Britain is to remain strong and able to project its values in 'The Asian Century', we need the European Union as a component in our foreign policy. It is certainly imperfect and in urgent need of reform. But, for all its faults, it is one of the biggest shows in town, and we should be on the stage.

———————————

I have heard conservatives call the Commonwealth "the network of the future". It is many things, some of them good, but I would not describe it in these terms.

It is more useful to acknowledge that the Commonwealth is somewhat of an anachronism but to recognise that it can still serve a purpose. What, after all, really links Canada with Vanuatu, or Lesotho with Malaysia? Not a lot. And many Commonwealth members remain frustratingly impervious to our liberal values. The retention of the death penalty and the criminalisation of homosexuality, ironically both policies promoted by Britain when we exercised direct rule, have almost become articles of faith for many Commonwealth members who will not countenance change.

The Commonwealth does have some powerful members, including five G20 countries (Britain, India, Canada, Australia and South Africa). But it would be perfectly possible for Britain to promote good relations with these countries without the existence of the Commonwealth.

So if the Commonwealth did not exist, there would be no clamour to create it. But it does exist, and there is no need to disband it. It is not our greatest foreign policy priority, but it is another tool in our toolbox, and a very distinctive one.

The Commonwealth does add up to more than the sum of its parts. Like a family, there is a familiarity, and sometimes a resentment, born out of a shared past. Diplomacy is, in large part, about creating and strengthening bonds with other countries, so it would be perverse to sever those that already exist.

The Commonwealth gives Britain reach into parts of the world where our influence would otherwise be more shrunken. There is no club with a substantial grouping of African nations that also has America, China, France or Germany as a member.

And, although this is a retro-fitted rationale for embracing the Commonwealth, it does include India as a member. The giants of 'The Asian Century' will be China and India. These two and America will be the three great economic powerhouses of the mid-century. By then India will have the largest population in the world.

We should seek to understand China better, but it is not a relationship that always comes naturally to Britain. There are too few shared references, a limited historical overlap and a shortage of contemporary cultural connections.

India and Britain, by contrast, almost struggle from having

too many shared references. We have to avoid being so over-burdened by our overlapping history that we lose sight of the great potential for future collaboration. We have an instinctive relationship with India. Given that we also enjoy a natural affinity with America, Britain starts ahead of the gain-line with two of the three great twenty-first century powers.

Whereas there is a lively debate about British membership of the European Union, and to some extent about the viability of the Commonwealth, there is no dispute that Britain should remain a member of the United Nations. The main discussion is about how that institution should be reformed, and what Britain's role within it should be.

There is always a tension, when determining the optimum size of an organisation, between inclusiveness and decisiveness. The more people who are consulted, the less that gets done. But the whole point of the UN General Assembly is that it includes all nations. It is the global forum. The main value of the meetings is that everyone attends them.

It is in regard to the Security Council, and specifically the five permanent members, where the scope for institutional reform exists.

The current permanent five – America, Russia, China, Britain and France – represents a hierarchy that is dated but not entirely anachronistic. Russia is a diminished successor to the Soviet Union. Britain and France are medium-sized countries in population terms, but are both in the top six global economies, and are both substantial diplomatic and military powers.

It is important that the United Nations retains credibility in a fast evolving world order. At the same time, membership of the

Security Council cannot be thrown so open that it ceases to be a plausible vehicle for addressing international disputes.

The candidates for inclusion in an expanded security council are mainly obvious. Japan and Germany, currently the third and fourth biggest economies in the world[105], are absent for historical reasons that no longer apply. India and Brazil are two bigger rising powers, and would provide a greater geographic spread, although the case for their elevation is certainly not accepted in Pakistan or Mexico. That leaves one continent, Africa, without representation, but without an overwhelmingly obvious nominee (South Africa and Nigeria insist there is an ideal candidate, but disagree about which of them it is). Enthusiasts for reform, with a Security Council expanded from five to ten permanent members, fudge this problem for the moment, only committing vaguely to some form of "African representation".

I find the case for expansion pretty compelling. The new ten would reflect the world as it is today.

The problem, however, with expanding the numbers is the increased scope for disfunctionality. This is already a big issue. The entirely understandable public reaction, in Britain and America, against the way in which the case for the Iraq War was prosecuted, has led us to make a fetish of Security Council Resolutions, as if all moral authority emanates from UN headquarters in New York.

That could be laudable in theory, but the effect is to give China and Russia, two countries with appalling records on human rights, the ability to veto enlightened liberal foreign policy interventions which they believe may threaten their self-interest.

Given that this in-built disfunctionality already exists, it is possible to argue that little harm would be done by adding five extra permanent members. I am not so sure. What characterises all of the potential new members, to varying degrees, is a strange inability to take decisive foreign policy decisions. They all want the prestige of being at the top table, but often so they can abstain in person. That is not a recipe for getting very much done, and, when unspeakable crimes are committed against defenceless civilians, an ability to get things done really matters.

It would also be a mistake, for the same reason, for Britain and France (and Germany) to forfeit their places to accommodate a European Union seat. These countries may not always agree with each other, but they do at least agree with themselves. There is already plenty of scope for institutional inertia as it is, without creating a place for an institution that often has no settled view.

The best solution, I suspect, may be a compromise: a new permanent ten at the Security Council, but with only the existing permanent five having a veto.

The United Nations will be a better organisation if it reflects in its structures the rapidly changing nature of the world order, with greater Asian representation, and a Latin American presence, at its highest level. But it needs also to demonstrate a capacity for leadership. Striking this balance will not be easy, but fixed adherence to the status quo risks the organisation gradually becoming a relic of a by-gone era, with declining legitimacy in the eyes of the emerging powers.

The advantage that NATO possesses is that it is constituted of like-minded countries with a clear shared interest. The Cold War that gave rise to its inception may have ended a generation ago, but it remains relevant to our security needs today.

It does seem highly unlikely that Britain will fight a future war alone. It is possible, in very limited terms, but we are right to see our modern defence interests as being tied to our closest allies. That requires us to retain a close working relationship with America, the pre-eminent military power, and to make a substantial contribution ourselves to the capacity of NATO.

It is not reasonable for European countries to have pacifistic levels of defence expenditure but retain America as an insurance policy in case their complacency about security turns out to be misplaced. NATO, as a tried and tested organisation trusted by the Americans, should remain our priority, not a European Union defence force with a dubious ability to act decisively, but we should continue to develop close collaborative working relationships with other European countries. France, as the only other European country with a substantial defence budget, is rightly our main European alliance.

The rapid change taking place in Asia is exciting, largely benign and advantageous to billions of people. But it is not without risks. The rise of China is changing the dynamic in Pacific Asia. The potential for heightened tensions are clear, with both Japan and South Korea attaching enormous importance to their support from America. China's ambitions in the South China Sea are controversial and resented. So much so that they actually provide a diplomatic opportunity for Britain with South East Asian countries looking to find new allies with clout on the world stage. The stand-off between India and Pakistan, meanwhile, continues.

Britain cannot and should not intervene militarily in these disputes, but we have a real interest in them. The stability of Asia is becoming increasingly relevant to our prosperity. So we need to remain a significant global player, and a key member of NATO, as well as an active participant in the European Union, Commonwealth and United Nations.

The alternative is that the new world order establishes itself with Britain left as a bystander. We owe it to ourselves, and to those around the world who look to us for leadership and support, to be more ambitious.

Nelson Mandela's public funeral service, in the stadium in Johannesburg, was attended by a stellar array of Heads of State and Heads of Government.

All of the three main British party leaders were there. So were the President of France, the German Chancellor and, memorably, the Danish Prime Minister. The British media portrayal of the funeral, and indeed Mandela's whole life, was that this was a central part of *our* history. The BBC's weekly Question Time debate was even broadcast from South Africa. A whole day was put aside in the British House of Commons for tributes to the late President.

And yet, looking at the international figures invited to speak at the funeral, what was striking was how differently the South Africans seemed to see things. Not only was the British Prime Minister not on the speakers list, but no European featured at all. The six international speakers invited to contribute did, however, include Vice President Li Yuanchao of China, President Mukherjee of India and President Rousseff of Brazil.

The world is changing. New foreign policy relationships are being forged, and new hierarchies established. When Mandela was released from prison a generation earlier these would not have been the countries pushed to the fore at such a major international event. Today they are. The lingering consolation for the traditional Western powers is that their sole speaking representative, President Obama, best captured the essence of the occasion and spoke most effectively for the wider world. It was an important reminder of the West's enduring appeal and influence.

The different cast list on this occasion sums up our foreign policy challenge in the new world order. For decades the choice facing all countries on big issues has been essentially binary: do they agree with the established Western powers or do they not? But in the short space of time between Mandela's release and his death, global power has shifted and new poles of influence have emerged. The world has already changed.

We – Britain and the West – can still speak for the world. Our open democratic culture and confidence continue to give us a competitive advantage compared to a country like China.

But we will have to work hard to be a force in the future. Our old alliances and old assumptions will not be sufficient. We will need to learn about more countries and cultures if we are to prosper in the networked world. In our foreign policy, as with all aspects of the global race, we will need to adapt in order to succeed.

Chapter eight
Government and the public services

An efficient and reformed public sector is a prerequisite for Britain being competitive in the global race. That reform should be guided by two core objectives: responsiveness and value-for-money.

In the largest emerging economies – China, India, Indonesia and Brazil – governments are faced with the daunting task of attempting to provide basic services for their whole population. With any service delivery, the quickest and most simple way to get up-and-running is to adopt a limited, uniform and centralised system. It does not take long to design a one-size-fits-all model. This was essentially the conclusion that Britain arrived at when confronted with the need to provide new services fit for heroes and their families in the post-War era.

This old model of public service provision is simple: a comprehensive, uniform service is designed, funded and delivered by the State. The citizen's role is entirely passive; there is no flexibility or scope for individual expression, everybody gets what they are given. How that service is structured – and how, where and when it is provided – is for politicians and bureaucrats to decide. Decisions, and funds, flow downwards from the top. Schools and doctors' surgeries are, in effect, outposts of the central State.

If we are to respond to the higher expectations of an increasingly well-informed population accustomed to making decisions, this historic model needs to be turned on its head. Where a person goes to school, when they see their GP, what sort of care they wish to receive in their home, how they wish to give birth or prepare for death; in a liberal society, all of these decisions should be taken by the citizen, not the State. The task then is to restructure our public services to allow the varied preferences of users, rather than the interests of providers, to shape the system. We need to create a "Doctor, the patient will see you now" culture.

Not only will this cultural change prevent public services becoming anachronistic or even obsolete in an era of diversity and choice, but it will also provide Britain with the competitive advantage that we need in order to succeed. This is not reform for the sake of reform. The goal is for Britain to have the best educated children, the best treated patients and the best cared for elderly people. We should not stand still while other countries catch us up and then overtake us. We need to innovate so that our population receives the best services in the world and our country is at the front of the global race.

The first and most fundamental shift required if we are to make services more responsive is to establish a culture of choice. This would send a clear signal that the default assumption in service provision is that the wishes of the user must be respected wherever possible. The ambition should be to move decisively and irreversibly beyond the old take-it-or-leave it model of service delivery.

The second change needed is the active encouragement of diversity and plurality. It was Henry Ford who famously said that his Model T car could be painted any colour "so long as it is black". This same attitude has essentially guided the provision of public services. In an age when a person can buy fifteen different types of coffee, customers are not going to settle for such limited choice, whether in the public or private sector. If they cannot get what they want from one provider, they will, quite understandably, want to go to another. Policy makers should make that possible. After all, no two people have exactly the same needs, circumstances, preferences or expectations. We need public services that both reflect, and cater for, these differences: different types of service, delivered in different ways, by different providers. We should let a thousand flowers bloom.

The decision about who should be allowed to provide a public service should be taken purely on the grounds of competence. If a provider agrees to deliver a service in accordance with the rules – publicly funded and accessible to all – the only additional test should be quality. Minimum standards should be set by the government and must be exceeded, but the decisive judgement should be left to the public. People will flock to the best providers and shun the worst; raising performance quality in the process. That is as it should be.

Third, if we are to empower individual service users, we need to allow them to hold the two controlling levers that, under the old model, were jealously hoarded by politicians and public service managers: money and information. Money to buy what they want; information to ensure that the money gets well spent. In some cases – nursery provision, schools, adult social care – this is best done directly, either through vouchers or individual budgets. In other cases, like complex medical procedures, this is best done through a decentralised commissioning process, where a trusted professional like a GP, ideally with a detailed knowledge of the patient, buys in services on their behalf. In all cases, however, the same principle applies: money should be pushed down to the lowest practicable level and then flow back up – the polar opposite of how funds have traditionally flowed through the public sector.

But this purchasing power will count for little unless it is accompanied by accurate, up-to-date and easy to use information. That is why on-line information sources like school performance tables, and websites like the School Data Dashboard, 'FE Choices' and 'Unistats' are such powerful innovations: they guide choice and put the individual in control.

Fourth, we need to decentralise services to the greatest possible degree. What works in one community, or in one part of the country, may not work in another. Moreover, what people value most in one place may differ from what people value most in another place. Nothing is as symptomatic of the post-War mind-set as the charge that geographical disparities create a "post-code lottery". Centralisation and standardisation – the hallmarks of nationalised services – are precisely what we are trying to get away from. The public services we will need in the twenty-first century are decentralised and diverse.

Fifth, in liberalised, choice-based systems, competition is unequivocally a force for good. It rewards success and ruthlessly exposes failure, creating a ratchet effect that drives standards ever higher. Monopoly provision, by contrast, cushions providers from the consequences of failure, leading to complacency and a lowering of standards. The new Competition and Markets Authority has rightly argued that market competition can help drive service improvement and value for money in public services. Applying competition rules to public services should be a priority for the new Authority.

Sixth, to make sure that competitive, choice-based markets function to everyone's advantage, not just those with the thickest wallets or the sharpest elbows, government should take deliberate steps to make those markets work in favour of those who need the greatest assistance. The pupil premium, the Government's school funding top-up system which allocates additional money to deprived pupils, already provides the template. I would like to see government grants to institutions replaced, wherever possible, with vouchers or personal budgets for service users. But I would also like to see those vouchers and budgets weighted in favour of the most disadvantaged. If all other things are equal, the most vulnerable could find themselves at the back of the queue; by giving them greater purchasing power, the government can ensure that the system performs well for everybody. Adopting such a system would represent the very best of social liberal thinking: delivering progressive outcomes using individualised, market-based mechanisms.

The final principle that should guide the effort to make our public services more responsive is personalisation. The revolution in information technology makes it possible for providers to tailor their services to the unique needs of the individual in ways that could not have been imagined just twenty years ago. The use of data as a diagnostic tool now allows teachers to tailor their instruction to the aptitudes and abilities of particular pupils, and gives doctors invaluable information on the lifestyles and medical histories of their patients. And by involving people in the design of the services they use – giving them 'voice' as well as 'choice' – we should be able to deliver ever more bespoke services, designed around the particular needs and circumstances of the individual. Mental health, special educational needs and adult social care services are all moving in this direction.

With the public sector accounting for almost half of our economy, Britain has no realistic option but to embrace reform. The delivery of responsive public services should ensure that reform – if we show the ambition and resolve to deliver it – supports our national strategic goals: higher quality service provision that results in a healthier, more highly skilled, more self-reliant and more productive population.

———————

Greater responsiveness must be accompanied by greater value-for-money. When resources are scarce, we need to do everything possible to ensure they are not misallocated or wasted.

It costs £2 billion every single day to finance Britain's public sector, taking public services and benefits together. Much of this money could be better used or even saved. Obsolete parts of government expenditure are allowed to linger due to passive political management and the protection of producer interests. Different governmental functions are replicated because duplication nearly always causes less controversy than rationalisation. Chronic inefficiency goes unaddressed due to a lack of transparency or accountability.

The size of our deficit and our debt means we literally cannot afford a business as usual attitude. David Cameron has said that "we have to be completely focused on getting more for less in our public services"[106]. I agree with that, but I would go further. We also need to consider where the role of the State can be reduced. Flabby and unnecessarily intrusive government is a burden we cannot afford if we want to make the successful transition to being a competitive and prosperous country in a dramatically re-cast global hierarchy. We need a more responsive State. But we also need a smaller and more efficient State.

———————————

I have never come across any business that measures its success by the amount of money it spends. Yet, all too often, that is precisely what the government does. Increased financial commitment to the NHS is provided as proof of emotional commitment to universal health care: I spend, therefore I care. In the private sector, the entire mind set is different: outcomes are everything; what matters is the service received by the customer. It has taken the biggest private sector suppliers years of meticulous and imaginative reform – raising standards and reducing unnecessary costs – to make a reality of this objective. We can learn from their journey.

I remember doing the weekly supermarket shop with my mother in the 1970s. We would file past empty shelves where the bread and milk should have been, with the staff unable to tell us when the next delivery would arrive. Without barcoding and loyalty cards, the supermarket had no real understanding of what their customers wanted. The stock-taking, supply-chain management and check-out service was primitive. Discounting was haphazard, shortages and waste commonplace, and the range of goods extremely limited. The stores were badly designed. There was certainly nowhere to change a baby or have a cup of coffee. Queues were long and customer parking inadequate. And, to top it off, they were closed in the evenings and on Sundays – the times when people with full-time jobs find it most convenient to shop.

By contrast, the public services of the 1970s are clearly recognisable to a person looking back from 2014. Of course there have been some technological advances and some infrastructure improvements, but the basic service is largely familiar. GP waiting rooms look similar; booking a GP appointment seems similar; GP opening hours are similar. Many hospital wards look similar; the hospital food might have improved a bit. School opening hours remain much the same.

What makes this more than an exercise in nostalgia is this observation: the surge in supermarket performance has been accompanied by a fall in prices, while the relative stagnation in the performance of our public services has been accompanied by a relentless increase in public expenditure.

In 1974 British households spent 24 per cent of their total income on groceries. In 2012 this had fallen to 17 per cent[107]. The cost of groceries in Tesco fell by a third in real terms between 1975 and 2007[108] while their range of products increased ten-fold. That is a remarkable improvement in performance which has had a transformational impact on the cost of living. By every measure of customer satisfaction, quality has soared.

The cost of running our school system, meanwhile, has doubled in real terms over the past 25 years, while academic attainment has flat-lined over time and declined relative to other countries. Total spending on the NHS has doubled in real terms in just the past 15 years.

I am not suggesting that running a school can be directly compared with running a supermarket. What I am suggesting is that we should not hide behind the differences and claim that there are no lessons the public sector could learn about delivering better services at lower cost. There are plenty, and we should learn them.

The first lesson from the private sector is that what matters is the bottom line. In the private sector, that means meeting customer demands in order to increase profitability. In our public services, that means educational attainment, employment levels, crime rates and so on. The relentless focus must be on achieving successful outcomes.

If we measure success in other ways, we will incentivise other activities. If the providers of a service are held to account for inputs – money spent, hours worked, forms filled – we will get what we deserve: a lot of money spent, a lot of hours charged for, a lot of forms filled. After all, what gets measured gets done.

If what we really care about is whether an adviser in a Job Centre is good at helping job seekers enter the labour market, we need to measure the number of people that adviser manages to move from welfare into work. If what we really care about is pupils achieving proficiency in the core academic subjects, we need to count how many are achieving the right grades in the right subjects at the right age.

It sounds easy but, in the public sector, it is harder in practice. People are rational, and the rational decision to make when your performance is measured by targets is to devote all your energies to hitting the target. So the Job Centre adviser will focus his or her attention on those job seekers with the highest skills and best prospects whilst ignoring those with a mental health problem or a criminal record. What is more, the adviser need not worry about how long the successful job seeker remains in the labour market before becoming unemployed once again; the target is to get people into employment, not into secure and sustained employment.

Similar problems have beset the school accountability system. If the government demands that a certain number of pupils demonstrate proficiency in a certain number of subjects, schools meet this demand in the most obvious way – by ignoring pupils who have already met the target, or who are unlikely to do so, and by ignoring those subjects that do not count towards the target.

These are not reasons to abandon the emphasis on outcomes, but experience has demonstrated that the system needs to be sufficiently sophisticated to avoid perverse incentives and results. Important refinements have now been introduced to make accountability systems more intelligent and harder to game. Hard-to-help cases count for more than easy cases at Job Centres. The progress made by all pupils across a broader range of subjects is now the focus of school performance measurement. And destinations data – the higher qualifications that students go on to achieve, the jobs they go on to do, the salaries they go on to earn – are increasingly being used to measure the value of Higher and Further Education courses.

The task for policy makers now is to iron out any further distortions that remain, and then to ensure that service providers are held properly to account – and, where appropriate, paid – according to outcome-based performance measures.

One area where liberal reformers should be particularly enthusiastic about linking payment to results is for the prison and probation services. Believing that incarceration should be about correction as well as public protection and retribution, liberals have long argued for a greater emphasis on prisoner rehabilitation. With the financial cost of locking up large numbers of prisoners impossible to ignore in an era of austerity, prison and probation officers are increasingly employed on a payment-by-results basis, with the desired result being a reduction in reoffending rates.

Thus, the politics of the heart and the head – an enlightened criminal justice policy and a prudent fiscal policy – have been aligned. The goal of rehabilitating prisoners before re-assimilating them into society has been hardwired into the system. It costs money to get a prisoner off drugs, to teach him a trade or help him find somewhere to live on release, but not nearly as much money as the cost of catching, prosecuting and incarcerating him over and over again. The incentives for the service providers are in harmony with the desired outcomes.

The second lesson from the private sector is that innovation and experimentation are the lifeblood of all efficient and well-run organisations. If an organisation keeps doing what it has been doing, it will keep getting what it has got. In order to achieve the objective of delivering more for less it is necessary to be willing to approach tasks differently. This is why outcome-based accountability systems and payment-by-results funding systems are so important; because they allow professionals the space and freedom to innovate in pursuit of agreed goals.

Politicians do not need to interfere in the methods used by service deliverers. With empowered public service consumers able to exercise informed choices, innovation and experimentation will drive a constant quest for performance improvement. When a particular approach has been shown not to work, it should be abandoned and another approach adopted. If service providers persist with ineffective methods of delivery, they will be exposed either by their superior competitors or, if they enjoy a monopoly or near-monopoly position, by the government's accountability system. The result is a constant upward pressure on standards.

The worst way to eliminate bad practice is for politicians to micro-prescribe inputs from Whitehall. Not only are they too remote from the problem, and too ignorant of the specific problems and challenges on the ground, but endless political interference saps professional morale, undermines professional autonomy and stifles innovation, leaving front line workers demoralised and disengaged.

A 2009 report for the Department for Business found, unsurprisingly, that organisations with engaged employees delivered higher performance and innovation. So it is worrying, and reinforces the case for intelligent reform, that public sector employees are less engaged with their organisations than private sector workers.

A survey by the Chartered Institute of Personnel and Development in 2011 measured net employee engagement with their organisation at -12 per cent in the public sector and +10 per cent in the private sector. The disparity in the leadership received by staff was even starker. Net employee satisfaction with managers was -10 per cent in the public sector and +28 per cent in the private sector. This may help to also explain the disparity in rates of absenteeism. Another survey in 2010 found that the average number of days lost per employee per year was 9.6 in the public sector compared to 6.6 in the private sector.

The lessons are clear. Public sector organisations, like private companies, and like the British economy as a whole, are only as efficient and productive as the people that work in them. Public sector workers are no different from any other workers; we all want to be trusted and valued; we all want to be given the freedom and responsibility to develop and grow; and we all want to work in dynamic, efficient and responsive organisations that deliver a high quality product or a valued service. Reform needs to tap into, not stifle, these instincts.

Achieving the optimum public service performance is also about understanding scale.

Improving value-for-money requires new thinking about the current structure of public services and whether money can be better spent without their provision becoming excessively remote from the user. Increasingly, it seems to me, the private sector delivers products and services on a big scale or a small scale, but rarely on a medium scale. Big offers economies of scale; small offers flexibility and customer proximity; medium offers neither.

Again the supermarkets – positioned on the cutting-edge of restless customer service improvement – provide an interesting model. The edge-of-town hypermarket has all the advantages of big: a massive range of products and the lowest possible prices. It may be a bit more of an effort to get there, but it is worth it for a big shop. The town centre micro-store has all the advantages of small: it is on the doorstep. The range of products is smaller and the prices are higher, but it is very convenient. The medium-sized suburban store offers neither of these outcomes as well, which is why they are becoming less common.

Similar considerations are relevant to public service provision. The constantly evolving search for greater efficiency and superior outcomes is a hallmark of all successful organisations. The alternative is that services are not modified even when they are offer poor value-for-money and cease to be aligned with public requirements.

Recent changes to police structures provide a strong example of commendable adaptability and illustrate the scope for further improvement.

In the first two years of this parliament the overall Home Office budget fell from £14.4 billion to £13.1 billion[109] and the funding for the police was reduced[110]. Yet crime rates continue to fall and are at their lowest level since the independent crime survey began in 1981. When making comparisons between police forces, what is striking is the absence of a correlation between changes to funding and changes in crime levels. Some of the sharpest falls in crime have been in police forces where the reductions in government spending have been greater than average.

Budget tightening has forced police forces to think more imaginatively about how they can improve their performance while still maintaining their core mission of protecting the public and detecting crime. Instead of trimming budgets across the board – so-called 'salami slicing' – many police forces have undertaken more fundamental assessments of how they allocate their resources.

In Avon and Somerset the number of Basic Command Units has been reduced. In Wiltshire the rank of Chief Superintendent has been scrapped. The objective is to reduce management and administrative costs without compromising the ability of the police to enforce the law. Across the board police forces are now co-operating in order to reduce costs, on everything from shared IT functions to uniform procurement.

This co-operation has taken place on a case-by-case basis but it has also been formalised by the enhancement of Regional Organised Crime Units. In the East Midlands (widely regarded as the best example) the five police forces are collaborating to fight serious and organised crime. The economies of scale that they have achieved, along with the sharing of expertise, means that people in the East Midlands have a more sophisticated level of police protection while, at the same time, less money is being spent than if each of the five forces were undertaking this work independently.

The best public service reform challenges the old assumptions about what constitutes a high-quality service at an efficient price. The police have succeeded in getting beyond the idle management style of submitting an annual budget request for 'inflation plus 2 per cent' whilst keeping exactly the same structure of service delivery. In an era of scarcity that is not good enough. We need to think not only about what we can afford but also about what we actually need to do at all, and if a task really does need to be done, how it can be done differently, better and cheaper.

But the evolving search for further value-for-money points towards the scope for further improvement. And it is in this spirit that I observe that there is not really a budgetary or management question in British policing for which the answer is "Warwickshire" or "Cambridgeshire".

I make no specific criticism of those forces, and could have picked many others to make this same point: no-one seeking to design from scratch the most effective and efficient system of policing for England and Wales could possibly arrive at our existing 43 force model.

The shire county force size offers neither the economies of scale and the concentration of expertise that a larger force would provide nor even the ideal supporting framework for the community-level engagement that is so effective at tackling crime at source. Only the larger forces possess the ideal critical mass; the remainder are unsatisfactorily medium in scale.

A national force would be too unwieldy, and its vast size would require it to be broken up, for internal management purposes, into smaller units in any case. A national crime fighting capacity is necessary but that is now provided by the new National Crime Agency.

The optimal structure would see the 43 different forces amalgamated into 10 to 12 regional forces, each of which would be roughly the size of the Metropolitan Police in London and the new single police force for Scotland. They would not necessarily need to replicate existing government regions; patterns of criminal activity would be a more logical basis for determining boundaries.

The cost savings would be considerable (a quarter of the number of chief constables, a quarter of the number of force headquarters) and the capacity to fight high-level organised crime would be enhanced. The National Crime Agency could more easily connect its operations with a smaller number of better resourced and more capable regional forces. The number of Police and Crime Commissioners could even be reduced without provoking a public outcry.

Under these larger force umbrellas there would remain a critical role for neighbourhood policing. With a less top-heavy management structure, greater shared internal expertise and less institutional clutter, there should be scope for an enhanced focus at this level.

This is not change for the sake of change. Crime, like business, is also constantly evolving, and usually at a faster rate than the public sector. It too has a tendency to gravitate towards the big (drug smuggling, people trafficking, organised internet-based fraud) and the small (anti-social behaviour, vandalism, late-night noise). We need to achieve better value-for-money but we also need a policing structure which tackles crime at the levels at which it poses the greatest threat.

The NHS also faces big/small/medium structural choices. The value of a big, specialist hospital, with a concentration of expertise, is obvious for any patient suffering from a complex and serious medical condition. Likewise, small, community-level health services are clearly the best way to deliver public health programmes like inoculations or screening tests. Instead, huge reserves of time and political energy are expended trying to protect medium-level service provision which provides neither the expertise nor the convenience.

Since Tony Blair was elected in 1997, the NHS budget has more than doubled in real terms, from £48 billion to £110 billion[111]. During that time, successive governments have attempted to inject a greater degree of competition and dynamism into the system. Yet, while the growth of the budget has been widely praised, almost every attempt at reform has been condemned. After the furore that surrounded the changes introduced earlier in this Parliament, politicians in all three parties are likely to back away from further reform, at least for the next five years.

Yet further reform is precisely what the NHS does need. The restless and innovative search for improvement is a distinguishing characteristic of successful organisations. Institutional inertia assumes that the existing money could not be spent any better and that our health outcomes could not be improved. That is not a safe assumption.

Comparisons of our health outcomes with those in comparable countries are not flattering. For example, the most recent measurement of five year survival rates for a wide variety of cancers – stomach, colon, rectum, lung, skin melanoma, breast, ovary, prostate, kidney and non-Hodgkin lymphoma – show that England performs worse in every single category than both France and Germany. For some cancers the survival rates are starkly different: kidney cancer, for example, where the five year survival rate in England is 47 per cent, compared to 64 per cent in France and 70 per cent in Germany[112].

Services are too often still orientated around the needs of the organisation, not the patient. This helps to explain why hospitals operate a skeleton staff at weekends and on public holidays. This means patients have to wait for the start of the working week to be treated, unless their condition is so urgent that treatment cannot be delayed. This is not just about the inconvenience and distress caused by delays; patients are statistically more likely to die if they are admitted to hospital at the weekend.

Treatment is rationed through delays. Hugely expensive equipment is under utilised, often sitting dormant in the evenings and at weekends. New technology is often slow to be made available, and sometimes ends up being funded by donations from voluntary groups. The quality of provision for people with acute care needs is variable and sometimes very poor. In extremis, patients suffer Mid-Staffs levels of negligence, which, to underline the scale of that tragedy, resulted in more deaths than the number of British soldiers killed in the Falklands, Iraq and Afghanistan wars combined.

Even if we could live with the NHS as it is today, it is doubtful that it can, without further reform, cope with the increased pressures placed on it by technological advances, the ageing of the population, and the growth of chronic, lifestyle-induced conditions. It is predicted that the number of dementia sufferers will rise from 800,000 today to over a million by 2021. 8,000 obese people received bariatric (weight loss) surgery last year, but 2 million people are currently heavy enough to meet the criteria for this surgery, which costs up to £11,500 per patient[113].

We cannot avoid the debate about where to draw the boundaries of free-at-the-point-of-delivery healthcare, and about which treatments might legitimately be subject to a charge. Nor can we avoid the debate about how we can best reform the service to ensure that money is better spent and in ways that make the

NHS more responsive to patient needs. We cannot ration more and more; we cannot tax more and more: we need new sources of revenue (mainly insurance payments) combined with a service delivery structure that ensures that money is spent efficiently in a patient-focused system.

Of course, it is much easier to resist change, do nothing and wish our problems away. But just as that was not the right approach when the NHS was introduced after the Second World War, so it is not the right approach today.

No area of government expenditure should be exempt from the search for better value-for-money, and that includes the cost of government and politics itself.

This may not be huge as a proportion of the overall government budget, but neither is it insignificant. In any case, it is imperative that politicians lead by example.

The structure of local government is a complete mess. There are different tiers (in some areas), elections by thirds (in some areas), executive mayors (in some areas) and anomalies such as Plymouth, the biggest place in Devon, not falling within the jurisdiction of Devon County Council.

In many communities residents pay taxes to fund their county council, district council and parish council. Few of them have any idea which council is responsible for which services. This undermines democratic accountability while the layers of administration add to costs. It also leads to a number of absurdities, such as one council being responsible for roads; another for pavements.

In an era of austerity, excessive institutional clutter feels like a luxury we can no longer afford.

Cornwall does not appear to have lost its Cornish identity or suffered a fall in service delivery standards by adopting a countywide unitary authority (although the number of councillors – 123 – still seems excessive). Even in Wales, where the fires of public sector reform rarely burn fiercely, the Williams Commission is expected to recommend a halving of the number of councils from 22 to 11, with most of the debate focusing on whether to go even further.

And if such a rationalisation of local government is desirable, then the same applies for national government.

We have too many government departments. It would be perfectly possible, for example, to disband the Department for Energy and Climate Change, with the responsibilities for climate change transferring to the Environment Department and the responsibilities for energy policy reverting back to the Business Department. And it is a patent absurdity, post-devolution, for there to be four separate departments for Scotland, Wales, Northern Ireland, and local government in England. The inability of the Cabinet to fit properly around the Cabinet table is a clear illustration of the problem.

And this process should not just include the politicians: the so-called 'Bonfire of the Quangos' has merely smouldered and warrants further endeavour.

The scope for cost-saving reform of Parliament itself is no less compelling, not by making elected office the exclusive preserve of the wealthy and political obsessives, but by reducing unnecessary expenditure.

The most radical solution would be to disband the House of Lords and move to a unicameral system. At the very least, there should be a cap put on the numbers of peers to prevent the party leaders conferring their patronage on ever more ex-politicians and major donors whilst requiring the taxpayer to foot the cost.

The House of Commons too could be reduced in size. The importance of maintaining a meaningful constituency link militates against a barbarous cut in the headcount. But – when seeking the right balance between maintaining effective representative democracy and achieving value-for-money – a reduction from 650 MPs to 600 or even 500 could be done. It would make sense at the same time to de-clutter the number of committees that exist primarily to keep MPs occupied.

All organisations, left to settle comfortably into their ways, start to silt up.

In the private sector there is a brutal corrective force: bankruptcy.

The on-going corrections which enable organisations to keep up with the times can cause difficulty. The skills of a particular employee may become obsolete; customers find changes to their routines disruptive in the short-term. But these evolving corrections are nothing like as painful as delaying and delaying until the choice faced is between a very large correction or the termination of the organisation.

In the public sector, these on-going corrections – the willingness to embrace innovative reform – are essential to prevent public support for collective provision being eroded to a level that threatens the social settlement on which all our public services are based. Enlightened change is an ally of the public services; not an enemy.

But the main point is this: if other countries have public services that deliver superior outcomes at a lower cost, Britain will be in trouble.

To succeed in the world, we need a health service that keeps people fit and healthy, schools that produce well educated and motivated students, an employment service that gives people the sense of self worth that comes from a job and a decent wage. We need probation, prison and social services that help people turn their lives around and contribute to society, early-years services that prepare children for school and allow mothers to re-enter the labour market, higher and further education institutions that help our young people to explore the many opportunities of the global economy.

And we need to do all of this while ensuring that, as a nation, we can afford to pick up the bill.

As the international competition intensifies, the slightly surreal debate about whether we prefer to have efficient or inefficient services will give way to a realisation that avoiding reform is impossible. There is no plausible alternative to being efficient and cost-effective. Responsiveness and value-for-money are the two reforming lodestars that will make our public sector perform to its maximum potential.

The global race is well underway. Time is not on our side.

Conclusion
2015 – Time to decide

There are two types of election: 'me' elections, and 'we' elections.

The first, in which the parties appeal to the immediate financial self-interest of the voters, are much the more common. Dangling bribes and blandishments in front of the electorate, politicians compete to offer more free or subsidised services to relieve pressure on household budgets. The debate is concerned with the short-term; the big and difficult choices are hidden away.

The second, in which the electorate is required to make an historic decision about the future direction of the country, occur very rarely. These elections are provoked by a realisation that the terms of the debate have changed fundamentally. Rather than politicians promising instant self-gratification, we collectively consider instead what shared qualities we will need as a nation to secure our long-term prospects. My contention is that we have arrived at just such a moment.

2015 should be a 'we' election, focused on the task of long-term national renewal. My fear is that it will be just another 'me' election, narrowly defined, focused on the here and now.

I think the British people, in the main, know that we are at a decisive moment for our country. Poorer than we were, weighed down by debt, with the forces of globalisation pounding at our shores and the entire world order changing before our eyes, there is an instinctive understanding that the decisions we must take, as a nation, are about more than the size of our utility bills.

If this parliament has been about repair and recovery, the next parliament offers an opportunity for reform and renewal. We must not let that opportunity pass us by.

Getting Britain fit for the global race is essential but it will not be easy or painless, which is why politicians, sensing our collective discomfort, go to great lengths to soften their message. But I suspect most people know, deep down, that their politicians are holding back from them the full magnitude of what is required. They might like the pill to be sugared, but they recognise that it must be swallowed.

If we are to deal with our deficit and our debt; if we are to reshape our public sector and reform our public services; if we are to reduce wasteful day-to-day spending so as to increase productive long-term investment; if we are to create a highly skilled workforce and a socially mobile society; if we are to foster a culture that encourages and celebrates enterprise and wealth creation; if we are to keep our markets open for business, engaging with, rather than retreating from, the outside world; if we are to lead in the world, exporting not just our goods and services but also our values, we need to not only hold to our course but also significantly increase our speed.

The danger, in 2015, is that we choose instead to change course, tempted by those who claim we can duck the difficult decisions that lie ahead. On the left we are regaled by a romantic social democracy, in which a re-inflated, unreformed and highly interventionist state will stand up to capitalist "predators" while making ordinary workers instantly richer; lowering prices, raising wages and slowing the pace of deficit reduction. On the right is a nostalgic nationalism, with the promise of a detached Britain, glorifying the past, fearful of the future, insulated from the fast-moving and unsentimental reality of globalisation.

If we are to succeed in 'The Asian Century', it is imperative that we avoid both of these easy temptations.

What Britain needs instead is liberalism, but with the handbrake released: an ambitious, confident, authentic liberalism. We must make the case for open markets, trade, migration, free enterprise and wealth creation. We need to eliminate the deficit, pay down our debts, encourage work, raise education standards, release the full potential of our population and invest in essential infrastructure.

We need to liberate our individual creativity and ingenuity. We must look forward not back; outward not inward; be curious and welcoming, not insular and defensive. We need to embrace the great challenge of our time with both self-confidence and humility. We need leadership, imagination and urgency.

If we do all this, Britain can lead the way in the global race.

Index

homosexuality 51, 171
Hong Kong 13, 87, 111, 115
House of Commons 33, 155, 161,
176, 198, 212, 213, 215, 217
HS2 120
hub airport 7, 61, 110, 111, 112, 113,
115, 116, 126
human capital 60, 83
human rights 9, 52, 152, 157, 169,
173

immigration 124, 148, 163
income tax 140, 145
independent school 85, 91, 92, 94
India 14, 16, 24, 25, 27, 29, 46,
47, 77, 124, 133, 150, 159, 160, 163,
164, 171, 173, 175, 176, 178
Indonesia 14, 16, 24, 28, 151, 160,
178
Industrial Revolution 5, 14, 16,
48, 66
international aid 46
International Herald Tribune 69
international institutions 52
internationalist 7, 24, 113
internet 66, 80, 122, 193
internship 61
Iran 155, 168
Iraq 49, 155, 173, 195
Israel 155, 168
Italy 15, 26, 37, 39, 50, 160, 161, 168

Jakarta 24
James Bond 22, 65
Japan 15, 16, 21, 26, 27, 35, 50, 87,
118, 151, 153, 154, 173, 175
Job Centres 187
Jubilee Line 108

Kabul 155
Kent 115

Laos 23
Latin America 14, 72
law 6, 42, 49, 51, 52, 71, 72, 138,
146, 152, 157, 191
Leeds 120
Lesotho 170
liberalism 7, 58, 59, 73, 74, 75, 77,
78, 79, 132, 137, 202
Libya 155
life expectancy 18, 36, 62, 124
Lima 111
Liverpool FC 37
Liverpool University 13
living wage 138
Li Yuanchao 176
Lloyd George, David 75
London 1, 10, 13, 17, 36, 42, 43,
63, 65, 66, 67, 71, 108, 110, 111,
112, 113, 114, 115, 116, 120, 121, 155,
160, 162, 193

M25 61, 115
Madrid 162
Magna Carta 71
Malaysia 106, 170
Manchester 110, 112
Manchester City FC 37
Manchester United FC 37
Mandela, Nelson 176
Manhattan 11
marriage tax break 141
Merkel, Angela 144
Metropolitan Police 193
Mexico 14, 16, 24, 28, 46, 72, 160,
161, 173
Middle East 52
mineral wealth 40
Minimum Funding Guarantee 101
Minister 1, 14, 15, 20, 28, 111, 157,
161, 170
Morocco 155
Moscow 155

Endnotes

1   Road Traffic Technology, "National Trunk Highway System (NTHS), China," *Roadtraffictechnology.com*, n.d.

2   "China High-Speed Train (Bullet Train)," *China Travel Guide*, n.d.

3   Dominic Wilson and Roopa Purushothaman, *Dreaming with BRICs: The Path to 2050*, vol. 99 (Goldman Sachs & Company, 2003), http://antonioguilherme.web.br.com/artigos/Brics.pdf.

4   British Council, "China: Facts," n.d.

5   *World Health Statistics 2013*. ([S.l.]: World Health Organization, 2013).

6   David Harrison, *Tourism and the Less Developed World: Issues and Case Studies* (CABI, 2001).

7   Travel China Guide, *China Outbound Tourism in 2012*, 2013.

8   International Monetary Fund, *World Economic Outlook Database*, Country/ Series Specific Notes, n.d.

9   Ibid.

10 Angus Maddison, *Contours of the World Economy 1-2030 AD: Essays in Macro-Economic History* (Oxford University Press, 2007).

11 Daniel Gros and Cinzia Alcidi, *The Global Economy in 2030: Trends and Strategies for Europe* (ESPAS, 2013).

12 Arvind Subramanian, *Eclipse: Living in the Shadow of China's Economic Dominance* (Washington DC: Peterson Institute for International Economics, 2011).

13 Organisation for Economic Cooperation and Development (OECD), "Medium and Long-Term Scenarios for Global Growth and Imbalances," *OECD Economic Outlook* 2012 (2012): 1.

14 United Nations and French Institute of Demographic Studies, *World Population Prospects: The 2012 Revision,* 2012.

15 National Institute of Population and Social Security Research in Japan, *Population Projections for Japan (January 2012)*: 2011 to 2060, 2012.

16 United Nations, Department of Economic and Social Affairs, *Old-Age Dependency Ratio*, n.d.

17 Office for National Statistics, General register Office for Scotland, and Northern Ireland Statistics and Research Agency, *2001 & 2011 Census* (ONS, 2011 2001).

18 International Monetary Fund, *World Economic Outlook Database*.

19 Ibid.

20 United Nations, Department of Economic and Social Affairs, *Old-Age Dependency Ratio*.

21 International Monetary Fund statistics based on gross Government debt: International Monetary Fund, *World Economic Outlook Database*.

22 Figures for 2002 and 2012 in US$ current prices: Ibid.

23 Stacy Davis, Susan Diegal, and Robert Boundy, *Transportation Energy Data Book: Edition 31* (Office of Energy Efficiency and Renewable Energy, U.S. Department of Energy, 2012).

24 Official Statistics for China found in: China Mike, "Facts about China: RICH, POOR & INEQUALITY," *China Mike*, n.d.

25 Shelter, "Average Earners Need £29k Pay Rise to Keep up with House Prices," *Shelter England*, n.d., accessed February 25, 2014.

26 Eurostat, *Population and Population Change Statistics*, 2012.

27 Rosemary Murray et al., E*migration from the UK* (Home Office, November 2012), 20.

28 Foreign and Commonwealth Office, "Thailand Travel Advice - GOV. UK," n.d., accessed February 10, 2014.

29 UK Border Agency, *Visa Applications to Be Simplified for Chinese Visitors*, n.d., accessed February 25, 2014.

30 International Aids Society, "Don't Forget Poverty" (Barcelona, 2002).

31 Kaleidoscope Trust, "SPEAKING OUT The Rights of LGBTI Citizens from across the Commonwealth," 2013.

32 International Monetary Fund, *World Economic Outlook Database*.

33 Office for National Statistics, *Gross Domestic Product Statistics*, 2014.

34 Department for Word and Pensions, *Tax Credit Expenditure in Great Britain*, January 2013.

35 House of Commons, *Parliamentary Debates (Hansard) Volume 574 No. 114,* 2014, 564.

36 Kevin Smith et al., "Crimes Detected in England and Wales 2012/13," *Home Office Statistical Bulletin*, 2013.

37 United Nations Office of Drugs and Crime, "Homicide Statistics 2013," 2013.

38 Department for Education, *Destinations of Key Stage 4 and Key Stage 5 Pupils, 2010/11* (Department for Education, June 20, 2013), 2.

39 House of Commons, *Parliamentary Debates (Hansard) Volume 575 No. 118*, 2014, 634.

40 Ofsted, *Latest Official Statistics: Maintained School Inspections and Outcomes* (Ofsted, December 5, 2013).

41 Organisation for Economic Co-operation and Development (OECD), *Programme for International Student Assessment Results, 2012*, 2012.

42 Organisation for Economic Co-operation and Development (OECD), *Education at a Glance 2013, OECD Indicators* (Organisation for Economic Co-operation and Development (OECD), 2013).

43 House of Commons, *Parliamentary Debates (Hansard) Volume 575 No. 118*, 284.

44 House of Commons, *Parliamentary Debates (Hansard) Volume 575 No. 116*, 2014, 47.

45 House of Commons, *Parliamentary Debates (Hansard) Volume 574 No. 115*, 2014, 673.

46 Ibid., 672.

47 Ofsted, *The Most Able Students: Are They Doing as Well as They Should in Our Non-Selective Secondary Schools?* (Ofsted, June 2013).

48 Independent Schools Council, *Attitudes Towards Independent Schools 2012*, 2012.

49 "Map of English Secondary Schools by Religious and Socio-Economic Selection | Fair Admissions Campaign," accessed February 25, 2014, http://fairadmissions.org.uk/map/.

50 Sandra McNally, "Report to the LSE Growth Commission: Education and Skills," accessed February 14, 2014, http://grammatikhilfe.com/researchAndExpertise/units/growthCommission/documents/pdf/contributions/lseGC_mcnally_edSkills.pdf.

51 Graeme Paton, "Just 17 'Incompetent' Teachers Barred from the Classroom," *Telegraph.co.uk*, 15:23, sec. educationnews, http://www.telegraph.co.uk/education/educationnews/8982966/Just-17-incompetent-teachers-barred-from-the-classroom.html.

52 John Burn-Murdoch, "How Have GCSE Pass Rates Changed over the Exams' 25 Year History?," *The Guardian*, sec. News, accessed February 14, 2014, http://www.theguardian.com/news/datablog/2012/sep/17/gcse-exams-replaced-ebacc-history-pass-rates?intcmp=239.

53 Civil Engineering Council, "Securing Our Economy: The Case for Infrastructure," 2013, 6.

54 Department for Transport, "Draft National Policy Statement for National Networks," 2013, 12.

55 Klaus Schwab, *WEF Global Competitiveness Report 2013-14* (World Economic Forum, 2013).

56 Department for Transport, *UK Aviation Forecasts*, 2013, 6.

57 HM Treasury, *National Infrastructure Plan 2013*, 2013.

58 McKinsey & Company, "Keeping Britain Moving: The United Kingdom's Transport Infrastructure Needs," 2012.

59 Windsor House Transport for London, "A New Hub Airport for the UK - Transport for London," accessed February 5, 2014, http://beta.tfl.gov.uk/corporate/about-tfl/how-we-work/planning-for-the-future/a-new-hub-airport-for-the-uk.

60 Oxford Economics, *Impacts of a New Hub Airport on Air Freight Industry, Customers and Associated Business Sectors*, 2013, 3.

61 McKinsey & Company, "Keeping Britain Moving: The United Kingdom's Transport Infrastructure Needs."

62 Ibid.

63 Ibid.

64 Ibid.

65 Environment Agency, "The Case for Change- Current and Future Water Availability," 2012.

66 Ibid.

67 John B Chatterton et al., *The costs of the summer 2007 floods in England* (Bristol: Environment Agency, 2010).

68 HM Treasury, *National Infrastructure Plan 2013*.

69 "Cisco Visual Networking Index: Global Mobile Data Traffic Forecast Update, 2012–2017," Cisco, n.d., accessed January 31, 2014.

70 David Dean et al., *The Internet Economy in the G-20: The $4.2 Trillion Growth Opportunity* (Boston Consulting Group (BCG), March 2012).

71 Ofcom, *Ofcom Infrastructure Report 2013 Update*, 2013.

72 Office for National Statistics, General register Office for Scotland, and Northern Ireland Statistics and Research Agency, *2001 & 2011 Census*.

73 National Housing Association, *Home Truths 2013/14: The Housing Market in England* (London, 2013).

74 Department for Communities and Local Government, "New Scheme Will Offer Hope to Millions on Housing Waiting Lists - Announcements - GOV.UK," February 14, 2011.

75 Office for National Statistics, *Index of Private Housing Rental Prices* (Office for National Statistics, 2014).

76 House of Commons, *Parliamentary Debates (Hansard) Volume 574 No. 114,* 547.

77 Amol Sharma, "Report: The Social Gains from Infrastructure," accessed January 31, 2014, http://blogs.wsj.com/ indiarealtime/2013/01/18/report-the-social-gains-from-infrastructure/.

78 House of Commons, *Parliamentary Debates (Hansard) Volume 574 No. 114,* 563.

79 House of Commons, *Parliamentary Debates (Hansard) Volume 574 No. 114,* 564

80 Office for National Statistics, *Gross Domestic Product Preliminary Estimate, Q3 2013,* November 2013.

81 Edmund Conway, "Britain No Longer Has the Worst Deficit in Europe," *Finance - Telegraph Blogs,* May 21, 2010, http://blogs. telegraph.co.uk/finance/edmundconway/100005840/britain-no-longer-has-the-worst-deficit-in-Europe/.

82 House of Commons, *Parliamentary Debates (Hansard) Volume 574 No. 114,* 564

83 Based on figures from United Kingdom Treasury, *Office for Budget Responsibility: Economic and Fiscal Outlook* (London: TSO, 2013).

84 House of Commons, *Parliamentary Debates (Hansard) Volume 574 No. 114,* 564

85 Ibid.

86 KPMG, "Corporate Tax Rates Table," August 26, 2011.

87 International Monetary Fund, *World Economic Outlook Database,* Country/ Series Specific Notes, n.d.

88 House of Commons, *Parliamentary Debates (Hansard) Volume 574 No. 114*, 654

89 International Monetary Fund, *World Economic Outlook Database.*

90 United Kingdom Treasury, *Office for Budget Responsibility: Economic and Fiscal Outlook* (London: TSO, 2013)., 14

91 James Browne, Andrew Hood, and Robert Joyce, "The £10 Billion Question: Where Could the Chancellor Find Welfare Cuts?," *Institute for Fiscal Studies: Observations,* n.d., http://www.ifs.org.uk/publications/6362.

92 Leandro Carrera, *The Implications of Government Policy for Future Levels of Pensioner Poverty.* (Pensions Policy Institute, 2011).

93 Quentin Peel in Berlin, "Merkel Warns on Cost of Welfare," *Financial Times*, December 16, 2012, http://www.ft.com/cms/s/0/8cc0f584-45fa-11e2-b7ba-00144feabdc0.html#axzz2sGawZLDR.

94 Ryan Bourne, "The Progressivity of UK Taxes and Transfers" (Centre for Policy Studies, October 2012).

95 Ibid.

96 ONS and Foreign and Commonwealth Office, *UK Trade 2013*, 2013.

97 "Speed Is Not Everything," *The Economist*, January 2, 2013, http://www.economist.com/blogs/theworldin2013/2013/01/fastest-growing-economies-2013.

98 All found in World Bank, *Economic Mobility and the Rise of the Latin American Middle Class*, 2012.

99 Trading Economics, *Brazil Retail Sales Year On Year*, n.d., http://www.tradingeconomics.com/brazil/retail-sales-annual.

100 Department for Business Innovation & Skills, "UK Trade Performance Across Markets and Sectors," *BIS Economics Paper* 17 (February 2012).

101 Embassy of Brazil in London, *Bilateral Trade: Brazil-United Kingdom 2012*, 2012.

102 William Hague, Foreign Secretary: Britain's values in a networked world, September 15, 2010.

103 Stockholm International Peace Research Institute, *Military Spending Database* (Stockholm International Peace Research Institute, 2013).

104 Hague, Foreign Secretary: Britain's values in a networked world.

105 International Monetary Fund, *World Economic Outlook Database*.

106 David Cameron, Prime Minister's speech on modern public service, January 17, 2011.

107 ONS Family expenditure survey, living costs and food survey: ONS, "Family Spending," *Office for National Statistics, Z.*

108 Stay informed today and Every Day, "One to Ten," *The Economist*, n.d., accessed February 14, 2014.

109 HM Treasury, *Public Expenditure Statistical Analysis*, October 2013.

110 House of Commons, *Parliamentary Debates (Hansard) Volume 574 No. 112,* 2014. 380

111 House of Commons, *Parliamentary Debates (Hansard) Volume 574 No. 114.* 590.

112 Roberta De Angelis et al., "Cancer Survival in Europe 1999–2007 by Country and Age: Results of EUROCARE-5—a Population-Based Study," *The Lancet Oncology* 15, no. 1 (January 2014): 23–34, doi:10.1016/S1470-2045(13)70546-1.

113 "Two Million 'May Need Weight Op,'" BBC, January 17, 2014, sec. Health, http://www.bbc.co.uk/news/health-25766253.